Introduction:

Methylation, Awareness, and You, "The Newly Unified Science of Health." A book discussing the new, Quantum Based Science of Methylation and Wellness that is sweeping the developed world in quantum leaps.

Read this and find that you can transform your body and mental well being in ways previously unknown to modern medicine and none of this requires an operation, any invasive therapy, or anything harmful. In fact, all side effects are additive!

This is not just an idle comment, but proven by the author and his friends and family and reiterated by those in the Yahoo Coconut Oil health group (4000 in all) that have put them in action. Some, as far away as New Zealand, have reported overcoming life threatening diseases as well as overcoming joint pain and arthritis, where we started. However, those without serious health issues have found that these protocols and techniques just bring a new level of energy and a newer, more inspired outlook to their lives as they have added and helped build on what I reported in my first book.

Welcome to my second book on many of the topics below with new ones that tell us some new technical reasons for why the protocols of my first book, "It's the Liver Stupid," worked so well for those who have read it and tried them.

**Kind Regards,
James Robert Clark
(HUuman)**

Table of Contents:

Introduction	
Foreword	4
Background	6
Methylation and the Protocols	8
HL MSM - History	9
Let the New Science Begin	10
Protocols: Limitations and Expansions	11
The Three-ringed Circus	13
GSH	15
Genetic Sequences: SNPs	16
Prenatal Care and Genes	18
Epigentics: A Spiritual Interchange	20
The Mechanics of Methylation	24
TMG: the Fatty Acid	27
HL MSM, Methylation, Epigentics, and More...	29
Universal Water Theory	32
Quantum Wellness: How It Ties In	36
Videography	37

Online Discussions (from Yahoo Groups):

(Group Post are in italics and all are edited)	40
Dr. Amy Yasko Genetic Panel Test	41
Dr. James Roberts	41
The Gut Factor/ Drugs	43
HL MSM... Reports... Side Effects:	44
Horse MSM... Always Best	45

Mark... Horse MSM Always Best	45
Fibromyalgia	46
Getting Better Gradually	47
Rates of Taking MSM	47
Mesothelioma... New Zealand (Wow!)	49
MSM is Not an Essential Food	50
Purchasing MSM & Discussion on MSM	54
Ketogenic Diet... Diet Discussions	**60**
What is this Ketogenic Diet?	62
My Goals as Opposed to Dr. Attia's	64
Dr. Mercola (introduced Attia)	65
Lyme Disease...	**66**
Vibrations in Diets	67
Beyond MTHFR	68
Drinking Ice Water	71
HL MSM Results	74
Nutrition...the Staff of Life	76
Moringa Leaf... Powerful Nutrient!	78
Buying Moringa Leaf	81
Vibratory Healing Techniques	81
Lab Crystals	81
Magnets	84
Beck Devices	93
DMSO	95
Himalayan Salt	99
Vit C Discussions	102
Transdermal Healing	129
Methyl B's could do harm	131

Which Whey?	**131**
Glutathione	**134**
Get the Genetic Test	**134**
Adapting to the MSM Taste	**136**
Thanks... And Another Healing	**139**
Niacin Vs. Niacinimide	**141**
Mainstream Tests Niacin... B-Vitamins	**144**
Methylation vs What Works	**148**
The Ultimate Quantum Machine	**150**
Agreements/ Closing Group Thoughts	**163**
Levels of Wellness: A New Realization	**184**
So What is Sacred: How it ties Together	**189-193**

Foreword

This book is mainly dedicated toward explaining this new Unified Medicine in nonscientific terms with powerful online references for those who want more, as it relates this new science to the three Protocols of my first book... especially the HL MSM Protocol. Using the ideas and terminology of methylation, it attempts to explain why people have had such profound results with them as we attempt to even improve those effects.

But also it also explains the Whey Protein and MSM, as we understand how genes interrelate with proteins, with methylation and organic sulfur, and how they can actually be a burden to a few as they attempt to employ them. These points are now more easily understood as we look at the evidence in solid, scientific terms that were unavailable during the writing of the first book.

Finally, the second half of this book gives you many online posts from members of the CCO online group on alternative health measures with my commentary. Some of this is new as it relates to the rest of the book and some was posted at the time, but all is edited to some degree, unlike the posts in the earlier book.

These posts are grouped conversationally to topics as much as possible. Readers will see some antagonism and resistance posted by otherwise open-minded people toward the idea that we no longer just throw nutrients at our bodies haphazardly. Now we see that this new medicine is truly outcome oriented and no longer about quantity. The idea here is to target problems based on tests and history, tests that were previously unavailable.

With this outcome based new science, I submit that nothing should be haphazard. However, we are all creatures of habit and slow to move to new ideas and methods. The idea behind this new science is to look at a person's history and their genetic codes (SNPs), then put them together in a designed program of organic nutrients as they adjust their attitudes to make it all work, as the videos in the last chapter teach us, so even the psychology is a giant step ahead.

The guessing game is over. Now we know why and how to do it. Still as discussed herein, the HL MSM (High Level Methylsulfonolmethane), UWPI (Undernatured Whey Protein Isolates), and LCD (Low Carb Diet) hold water for most people. Then, speaking of water, I suggest a new theory of why and how methylation and epigenetics works with water as the liquid crystal carrier and contributor as we move into thinking of water from the quantum viewpoint.

When it comes to genetics, none of this is simple and the further you go, the more complex it becomes. By the time you get through this book, the hope is that I will have spelled it out well enough and will have opened the door with some good references to turn to if you are interested in the more complex details.

Background

In the beginning, man lived a life of simplicity where his food mainly came as what is popularly termed by today's sociologists as a hunter gatherer. Over the past one hundred years, things changed dramatically mainly in how we obtain our food. The net result is that little that we eat has much food value. Additionally, there is the possibility that our water has become altered and no longer contains the high vibratory rates that it once did as Dan Nelson, the Quantum Physicist, claims at:
https://www.youtube.com/watch?v=7hNW7qxIMzg

The most obvious recent changes have been in our medical system, where large pharmaceutical companies have come to control our lives (with government backing). The net effect is herein referred to as Mainstream Medicine. This bent has literally driven many doctors from the profession as it has moved from healing to reducing symptoms.

In reaction to mainstream medicine, especially since the event of the worldwide web, we now have a thriving community known as "alternative health or naturopathic medicine."

These two groups until about 2010, stood in sharp contrast to each other. Mainstream medicine is based on conventional science/ Newtonian physics and disease treatment. While naturopathic medicine may also be scientifically based, it is often empirical in nature. Therefore, is generally outcome based and more directed toward overall wellness. Furthermore, today it delves into far greater depths than mainstream medicine explores and even goes into the quantum realm. Today, terms and concepts enter the picture like: fractals, methylation, epigenetics, and MTHFR.

This book, an outgrowth of my first book, "It's the Liver Stupid," takes the empirical practices that I discovered, what I called protocols, and looks at them in the light of what I see now as a Paradigm Shift in medicine. This began with the conventional scientific study of genetic sequences. It then merged with the findings that organic nutrients as well as certain spiritually based practices such as meditation, prayer, visualization, etc. Now known as Epi (or beyond) Genetics, it can cause the human body to avoid disease and likely lengthen our life spans to new levels.

I call this new level herein "the unified science of health," hence the subtitle of this book. It combines the concepts learned prior to genetics which led to the methylation pathways, with what I had discovered previously.

I am a moderator in the on-line health discussion group, the Yahoo Coconut Oil (CCO) group, and have been a member for more than ten years. Only recently have I become aware of the term methylation in the context of this new medicine that is blossoming across the developed nations of the world.

In bringing this out, I have become only too aware of what I see as a cultural lag within the alternative community and even those who pride themselves as naturopathic. In fact, I conjecture that this resistance would probably be as strong as the prejudice that the mainstream has held for the alternative people, were it driven by money.

Methylation and the Protocols

To begin, there are several things at play here that I discovered as I researched methylation, but the two protocols, HL MSM and UWPI are, first, both organic sulfur based. This is key; however, the more interesting thing is here is that the two methyl groups in MSM apparently acts as a supercharger for at least one of these cycles as the organic components interplay.

Even though several experts have discussed the methylation components, there is no researched proof that the methyl groups are the key element in our results at the point. Nevertheless, I hold it to be true given what has been reported in powerful anecdotal evidence and it now makes perfect sense. Finally, all fatty acids in the methylation sequences are comprised of organic sulfur in some form. By virtue of this new science, we can see that MSM and DMSO should have profound effects on health unless you have the expressed genetic predisposition to not use them as discussed.

HL MSM - History

So moving on, my interest in High Level MSM started when I was told that it would heal joint problems (and that proved out for me). However, what occurred beyond that was a complete shock to me, just as it was to all that I recommended it to. As it turned out, they came back with astounding healing reports.

At these high levels, the curing powers of MSM obviously begin to take on powers that no one had previously suspected. Keep in mind that no one who used this HL MSM protocol was ever told prior to using it that they would ever see these far-reaching results (placebo effect). This, then, is not mental expectation as nothing was anticipated other than joint healing.

These reports are becoming more common as time goes on, but below are some of the prime examples:

Pam in our group reported how her memory improved dramatically. Ann reported getting over fibromyalgia (as she says, this will take awhile), and Deanery of New Zealand reported that her husband's Mesothelioma was in remission (at least, maybe cured).

Finally, my past poster girl, Mona in CA, was virtually cured of the usually fatal autoimmune disease, PSC. With these, it became clear that this HL MSM Protocol apparently had a great deal more going for it than just as a supplement of organic sulfur, as I had presupposed. That is, in these high level amounts, what we have here is a mind-boggling health benefit that is pushing the mind and body to new levels of wellness. MSM is commonly used in three gram doses or less, but the word is getting out.

In my first book, I gave limited service to the methylation component of MSM. In that era, the methylation sequences were seldom even written about. While they were not well-known, they were interesting, nevertheless. However, as we discovered recently, this study has blossomed as we see to allow this Paradigm Shift in medicine to occur.

Let the New Science Begin

In studying the work of the Dr. Bruce Lipton, PhD, who wrote about this very topic in his book, *"***The Biology of Belief*** "* https://www.brucelipton.com/, termed epigenetics, we see how this all ties into the previous hard science of genetics that only emerged in the late '90's. This work is still in its infancy, but it is moving very quickly. Nevertheless, the genetics field is now mature compared to the methylation therapy that grew out of it. The history of genetic sequencing is covered well here: http://en.wikipedia.org/wiki/DNA_sequencing

There are several important cofactors in these cycles which are outlined in many places on the web, but MTHFR.com hosted by Lipton is the key place to find this information. He also lectures in free You Tube videos, so please, search and listen to him. Do not be intimidated by what he is saying. There are bound to be new discoveries, but you already have the most important part with epigenetics. The charts (diagrams) are helpful, are improving, and there are many on the web. Find a good one and bookmark it for reference, as you read this. Lipton's work is among the best.

When Paul in our CCO Group gave us a link to this new methylation therapy, the light went off for me. What I gathered immediately on reading what Paul had led us to was that MSM and whey revitalize these entire sequences in ways that most of these pioneers have yet to recognize. As noted above, I call it supercharging (as a gear head), but the effects are "that good."

While sulfur based, undenatured whey protein isolates (UWPI) help build Glutathione, one must assume that HL MSM adds to the entire sequence (again, all of the fatty acids in the sequences are sulfurs and MSM is one-part sulfur), so it makes perfect sense. Along with the Low Carb (Paleo) Diet, the three come together in a way that I could never have anticipated when writing my previous book. I see this now as either divine intervention or incredible luck, but it happened.

Protocols: Limitations and Expansions

While I was entirely unaware of the CBS restrictions below prior to learning this new science, as a firm believer in naturopathic methods (and, certainly, I gave weight to this in my first book), allow me more emphasis here, as we move along:

Protocols defined as set methods, amounts, and ways of doing things, in themselves, simply do not work. Given this new science, we see clearly why. The first law of this new "Unified Medicine" is that we are individual biological entities that require individual knowhow and attention. However, that said, these three proven methods commonly can be applied to most all who read this in very beneficial ways. That is, if we take the time and pay attention to body feedback and mental changes as they occur, and stay alert as they proceed... More on that later.

Nothing here can happen over night. This new science takes time and patience. No quick cures here, please. Reading the posts, you will see that people like Joyce M., to her credit, took a full year to arrive at her current MSM intake level as she adjusted her life to total wellness (at age 60, by the way). At this point, she has it figured out. Now, Joyce M. can be almost guaranteed a long and pain-free life.

In my first book, I thoroughly outlined the UWPI and HL MSM Protocols. There, I mainly left the explanation for the UWPI Protocol up to Duncan Crowe who formulated it from the work of the manufacturers of Immunocal,
http//www.immunocal.com/WebFlash/patient.wcp?&site=corp

a pure, proprietary, form of whey. The theory behind their findings was that regular use of UWPI aids in the production of GSH (Glutathione)**http://en.wikipedia.org/wiki/Glutathione** Immunocal holds several patents on their product. UWPI is mainly about increasing the GSH levels. More on that below.

I also outlined the history of how I came across the HL MSM Protocol from a Kentucky Horse Farmer who sold it on the web by the railcar load and why I always buy MSM in bulk that is intended just for horses. This is the best source. While you should never jump into a protocol with both feet, the intention is to finally be taking at least two heaping teaspoons of it a day and more is even better for many of us. As I say here and elsewhere, a half cup per day is not too much.

Interestingly, I recently ran across another horse farmer, Mark (post below in discussions), who verified this story. As another horse farmer nearby told me, we all know about this and we always take care of our horses. It makes you wonder why they don't all get onto to this HL MSM themselves, but she had not. Is she on it now? I have to wonder. I gave her the information.

The Three-ringed Circus

The HL MSM Protocol is known to work on at least one of the three methylation cycles, but quite possibly more, again, by supercharging the Methionine and reinforcing the Sulfur as needed.

More study needs to be done, but my theory here is that the effects are simply too good to be working as currently assumed. Furthermore, I hold that as we progress and the word gets out on this protocol. New studies, experiments, and discoveries will prove this three-cycle theory out. The money to do this is simply not yet available. The nutrient organic Vitamin C aids in this uptake of MSM and should be considered as essential to the protocol. So if C is missing or low, expect poor outcomes. I keep a good stock of organic lemons on hand and eat them skin and all. Sometimes it is blended and sometimes it is used as a simple snack.

Think of the methylation diagrams as a three-ringed circus. Each one functions independently, yet they interact to create the whole show. Obviously, any single one can be the main event and that is why our bodies are so powerful at self-healing. MSM may allow one ring to steal the show or it may be acting in the other two and that remains to be seen. GSH, the coordinator of the events, is making this all happen, but the double methylation groups of MSM and DMSO can easily steal the show if allowed. They are real performers, but the show will go on even without them and there are other ways to do this.

Most of our attention, as we watch, will be on the basic element in this show, organic sulfur. However, there are other things that can steal the show like Dan Nelsons "Wayback" Water. In fact, his water allows us to see this all occur in ways that we never dreamed possible as we discuss below (and Joyce reports in her post later).

The bottom line is that this show can actually get our attention at levels never previously understood and it can go on for much longer than most believe today. In fact, if we become really involved, we can creatively join in, rather than just be spectators. It's really great fun!

GSH

GSH, the master antioxidant, is the driver of the Pathways that move the cellular powerhouses, the mitochondria. GSH does all sorts of good things to keep you alive, as follows:

While GSH is not considered an essential nutrient for people because the body makes it, it is certainly essential to all life. Nothing, then, could live without it, just as nothing could live without methylation. The interesting thing about GSH is that, once it is oxidized (then called GSSG), it can be recycled, then reused by the various essential fatty acids to begin its work in a new cycle. The key here then is to keep this cycle repeating, so as to remove the harmful products, free radicals and oxygen species, from the system. The actual workings are well described in the above references, with charts for those interesting in learning these complex sequences. The liver is the primary organ of this work, as I discovered when writing my first book. However, it occurs in every live cell in the human body, in all plants, and fungi.

When, in the human body, the level of GSSH is higher than 10% of the available Glutathione, the term used to describe it is "Oxidative Stress." When this occurs, cancer, autoimmune, and other life threatening diseases cannot be overcome, thus the body and death of the cells can be expected unless relief comes. Environmental toxins can contribute to this cycle, but many other factors such as poor diet are huge. The lack of essential nutrients, or stress of any kind, can also contribute. The nutrient Selenium aids in GSH production and should be considered as essential to it. If it is missing or low, as is commonly the case, expect poor outcomes.

Reinvention: Finally, notice that GSH, like the transformation that occurs between as MSM and DMSO, reinvents itself. This is an otherworldly concept (part of the reason that I say that we are quantum beings) and why the UWPI is so valuable, as is HL MSM. Reinvention is common in plant biology, but almost unknown in humans except in this basic methylation cycle with GSH. Trees live for hundreds, even thousands of years, for this reason. Now we are introducing this concept into our human biological system with these two protocols and for the first time ever objectively.

Genetic Sequences: SNPs

More recently, leaders in the genetics field have come to realize that certain genetic breakdowns occur and they can happen virtually anytime in life. Importantly, we now have ways to measure and chart the various level of components in the methylation cycle (pathways) so that they can be analyzed and acted upon. Each of these areas are referred to as SNPs (say snips). Read about them at:
.http://www.snpedia.com/index.php/Single_Nucleotide_Polymorphism

Once you know where the defective SNPs are, that is, where the contributors are too high or low (either way, there are problems), you can make dietary, sleep, lifestyle and other adjustments to fix them. However, the history of the person with these problems can generally tell you well in advance of actual measurements.

Still, these methylation cycle chart readouts are valuable clues to why we are not doing well on certain diets and nutrients. A high reading in one area usually means a low uptake in another, but it could indicate too much supplementation of a single nutrient. The key to this new science is always balance. No longer should we indiscriminately take any single vitamin haphazardly. For the first time in the history of man, we actually have a methodology and a measuring system.

Listening to the healthcare experts: The most common SNP to show defects is the MTHFR sequence, CBS comes in at a close second, and COMT is third. However there are nine total gene sequences that can currently be measured objectively and all can have profound effects on your mental and physical health.

Additionally, there are some forty others that remain outside the scope of today's test labs. So there is plenty to learn in this field and it is all very new and quickly expanding. The promise here is that all known diseases may some day be mapped and treated with organic supplements, foods, various relaxation techniques, etc.

Don't become distraught if your SNPs turn out ugly because there is still the trump card, epigenetics, that I discuss in depth elsewhere. This can negate genetic expression entirely and this is actually spirituality, just as I introduced in my first book. This can override most any physical readout, no matter how bad it looks, and it goes well beyond the genes which can only effect proteins as Dr. Bruce Lipton and others discuss.

Looking at the MTHFR sequences (the enzymes are of the same name), we find that a person can have deficiencies on either side. This is true for all sequences. That is, there is one gene on each side (from mother and father) and should both show up as positive (which means bad in this case), the person is most likely going to have serious problems in this area.

If a genetic problem occurs on one side **(+/-)**, the related stress factor is now thought to be about 20% decrease in efficiency. A +/+ defect, meaning a defect on both sides would mean maybe a 60% loss or more according to the epigenetic influences that are unreadable. A defect can occur before birth or any time thereafter from stress.

Some question as to whether genes actually repair themselves, but Dr. Lipton and I say they do. This would relate to the past finding that it was assumed that brains and nerves could not self-repair, but now we know it all happens through epigenetics especially.

Prenatal Care and Genes

For the above reason, we must stress, even more, just how important prenatal care and nutrition are to the health of a mother and baby. Furthermore, any stress in life, from money problems to the death of a loved one, can cause a defect in a gene sequence, just as an exposure to any toxin from an airborne chemical to nuclear fallout (previously well known) can create a problem.

The bottom line is that stress can take on many forms and any can make you ill or eventually kill you if it is not relieved and, as noted, the gene defect can be repaired or compensated for with diet, etc., epigenetically. So you see now why my first book so strongly emphasized spirituality and love as avenues to overall health. These should be considered as important as any nutrient (far more so, really) to the health of an individual as I emphasized there. With a pregnant woman, given what we know, they certainly are all key issues.

So the above key elements stressed in my first book were correct. These same spiritual elements are now considered as key by these advanced epigenetic scientists. Thus they came through intuition and empirical reporting rather than measurable, observable facts as this new field of epigentics is now advancing.

The bottom line is, as the naturopathic doctor, Amy Yasko, MD., tests and advances. As an early mover in this field, she has set the stage for this new era in medicine. Now we can look at a problem and address it as we always have. But from here, we can now see measurable data that can, for the first time, give us rational proof of why it has occurred unless it was purely epigenetically related.

When all fifty of these sequences are understood empirically and logically, we will have entered the new paradigm that this predicts. The earlier protocols outlined in my first book somewhat predicted this with their methyl and sulfur groupings, but they missed on the fact that all cannot use these or any other nutrients equally.

Epigentics... A Spiritual Interchange

So now let us move back to my favorite topic here, spirituality. Again as discussed above, it is now for the first time in history predicted by actual clinical experience as these scientists report them. While this has been known to be true intuitively forever, let us delve further into its workings and actual definition as follows:

Epigentics can be defined as the study of inheritable changes in gene function that occur without a physical change in the DNA sequence. That is, it is the link between the environment and actual gene expression that is critical to your health. You possess thousands of genes and all are the same in each of your cells. However these genes are expressed or silenced differently in hundreds of cell types (heart, liver, skin, etc.) throughout your body. Therefore, epigenetics is now considered to be more crucial factor in cell differentiation and development than the actual gene sequence.

The web is now chock full of information on epigenetics and you could watch You Tube videos on it for days on end, but I recommend this Nova Video to get you started as it is particularly well done:
https://www.youtube.com/watch?v=D44cu7v9x1w

So we now know that genes can be shut down or expressed according to awareness and what we eat, drink, and our environment. So, for certain, we know that our attitude toward our daily experiences constantly changes. That is, how we respond to everything alters our expressed genetic profile whether negative or positive. So you produce all outcomes.

You can now say that a negative attitude will express a positive +/- gene profile and it becomes a physical part of your entire body and expressed throughout every cell. Who would have thought that an angry person could be creating bad genes that could stick with them forever? Or, conversely, that a loving person is changing genetic defects that can never be expressed? Wow! The bottom line here is that there is a memory marker in genes that recalls what has occurred or what we focus on in our lives. We control it by our thoughts and actions. Nothing in the past was so obviously expressed through behavior on a scientific basis. Furthermore, we now know that genes, are mostly the basis for mental illness. So, when we are angry, we invite both mental and physical problems.

So please allow me to turn this all around and look at it from the other viewpoint. The spiritual masters over the eons have told us that our loving thoughts influence us physically and even change our physical appearance. Now we have physical and scientific proof of what they were telling us. It's absolutely true. By this, from the above, you can actually physically repair genes as well as disrepair them, you can actually begin to perfect your body over time. So now that we know that genes affect us mentally, we know that there is a powerful physical and mental interchange in both directions.

Focusing on the positive side, this would mean that there is an actual physical/mental building or repair that goes on for those who keep a highly spiritual outlook. Furthermore, this expression even applies to nations and regions. That is, by keeping a good attitude, as the Italians do, a genetic MTHFR +/- genetic defect, almost universal there, is almost never expressed. However, in the US, this is commonly a huge problem. Knowing this to be true, one could say that in a real sense, all nations carry karma and this is expressed in their daily lives. Finally, we generally pay to live in this fast moving environment dearly in ways never before understood.

Now, more down to earth: In epigentics it has been found that a methyl B vitamin in the correct amount can physically silence genetic expression of a defective gene. So the key point here is that defects in the genetic readout are not nearly so important as manstream scientists had hoped when they finally sequenced the gene code. That is, all expressions can be neutralized by changes in diet, thought, and lifestyle. The SNP readings are changed by epigenetic masks or actual gene alteration per Dr. Lipton. This is the reason that all of our countermeasures work and, again, why attitude is such an important element when it comes to expression.

Now, relating this to the HL MSM Protocol: The epigenetic mask is expressed with help from the methylation process which is encouraged by changes in the various elements that encourage wellness. So, quite simply, the methyl "tags" can be changed. This alone could be the repair that our HL MSM protocol triggers and, this being the case, the actual genetic readout is of even less importance to us when we include this protocol. Still, always remember that the real trump card is how you live your life and this is most important beyond any other countermeasures, So go back to the related chapters in my first book and read the discussion on how we can change spiritually through the powerful visualization exercises. By looking at yourself as a loving being, you become loving. It is that simple, but there is more.

Finally, as the above Nova video tells us that through epigenetics, negative environmental tags cause diseases downstream from the actual exposure to an individual. What this means to you is that if your grandfather was present at a crop spraying, he could express a tag that could cause you to catch cancer fifty years later.

However, per the above, you are in luck: You can overcome your grandfather's unfortunate exposure by simply becoming more spiritually aware, or getting your house in order. Most importantly, with all of this new science and objectivity, you now know that you are in control of your outcome. You are not the victim that current Newtonian medical science would make you out to be. You are not a genetically controlled puppet by any means.

The Mechanics of Methylation

Now that we have discussed the spiritual aspects, we move on to a summary of the general mechanics of methylation (that I consider far less important):

The Role of Methylation

1. Turns genes on and off.
2. Removes toxins and heavy metals.
3. Removes environmentally caused genetic polymorphisms (and thus cancer before it develops).
4. Keeps you mentally stable and alert.
5. Is thus a key factor in all mental disease
6. Allows you to sleep soundly.
7. Keeps allergies and infections at bay.
8. Regulates its own enzyme and hormone sequences by

turning them on and off.
9. Reduces oxidative stress.
10. The Liver, as the master organ, talks to your body through methylation sequences.
11. Creates killer cells: T cells to fight viruses and bacteria.
12. Is key to the growth and repair of all cells.
13. Generally, heals you of any disease (it's not the drugs).

Methylation Inhibitors:

1. Birth Control pills.
2. Folic Acid in packaged foods... Most likely causes cancer (MTHFR.com).
3. Aluminum, iron, and heavy metals in the diet or absorbed through the skin.
4. Nitrous Oxide
5. High dose Niacin.
6. An excessive quantity of any supplements found in the methylation sequences.
7. The wrong supplement. Especially metallic metals and inorganic vitamins as commonly sold in packaged foods and daily vitamins.
8. Any genetic mutation/ polymorphism.
9. Depressed mental state.
10. Pharmaceutical Drugs. Nearly all, but certainly cancer and mental treatment drugs

Most everyone has one or more genetic defects and particularly in the MTHFR sequence. Dr. Bruce Lipton reports that he has only seen three charts that had no defects, so far, since he has been reading them. Any historical abnormality would indicate one or more defects, whether it is: migraine headaches, a tendency toward habitual behaviors such as fits of anger, alcoholism and smoking, problems in sleeping or a tendency to overreact to everyday problems. Nothing that we do or suffer from can be discredited that is out of the ordinary.

So these defects are rampant in current populations, but some populations show much greater occurrence than others. The Mexican, Italian, and Spanish populations have very high homozygous TT genotypes in the MTHFR gene, while the West Africans of Ghana and Ivory Coast score nearly zero across the board.

It will be interesting as time goes on as to why and how this finally plays out. As previously discussed, we are quickly discovering that the actual defect is far less important than the lifestyle of the person and population as a whole. Importantly, we must learn how the body actually disrepairs and repairs the gene sequences. This will be an interesting study, but, as we see, it is the actual genetic expression that is key to our health, wellness, and anti-aging factors. The bottom line here is that a bad attitude can, and probably always does, kill you.

TMG: the Fatty Acid

TMG (Trimethylglysine) http://en.wikipedia.org/wiki/Trimethylglycine is a particularly important fatty acid in the methylation process. TMG causes the reactivation of homocystein, which occurs in two of the three pathways. Up till now, those who have read alternative information on heart disease may be put off by the term homocystein. The fact here is that doctors have identified an essential part of the methylation pathway with heart disease, and somehow made it sound like a bad thing. And this is a common occurrence.

The point with all things in the pathway is that when any one is out of balance (and all parts can be), they become markers for problems in themselves. Likely, most Doctors in the past never had a clue just how special homocystein was, as it was seldom (or never) fully discussed in this sequence previously. So we enter this new era of understanding with methylation as awareness increases.

Does this sound familiar? Cholesterol comes to mind. I need not tell those who read my first book, but cholesterol was the first and biggest of these markers to make the mainstream bad-guys list. Furthermore, you know that the cholesterol myth has become a way to market statin drugs and has made billions.

TMG occurs in the foods primarily as outlined below.

However, by all means, if you can eat eggs without problems, eat them to aid in this process. I make them a part of my UWPI (Undenatured Whey Protein Isolate) mix that I eat three times a day. This mix includes two heaping tablespoons of whey (UWPI), a level spoonful each of Moringa Leaf Powder and Maca, a raw egg or two, and a couple of tablespoons of high grade cream from Golden Guernsey cows (Golden Guernsey A-2 cream is great stuff and about the consistency of butter, LOL).

The above and the HL MSM Protocol boost Methylation Processes which are key to every process needed to stay alive and thrive. Also, these all dovetail with the LCD (Low Carb Diet) as outlined in my first book (unless you happen to have a genetically expressed problem with sulfur).

Sugar Beets are a particularly simple source of TMG and, if you are like me and do not like them, it may be time to warm up to them some. They are helpful, cheap, and plentiful, but are too high a source of fructose to eat very often (and sugar does age us). Given this fact, the correct way to use them is to use the fermented juice, known as kvass. However, for those who are sensitive to oxalates, kvass may not be a good choice, in any case. Moreover, for TMG, there are better sources than beets, which are only about 1/3 as dense a source as spinach, so we are in luck. Your best sources for TMG are: spinach, lamb and goat quarters, kidney, liver, and other organ meats.

So TMG is extremely important in that it re-methylizes homocysteine and thus it is one of the key factors in how well the mitochondria function.

The cofactor supplements that may be considered relative to the sequence include: First, the B vitamins: Methyl B-12 (essential to the cycle), P5P B-6, B-3, B-2, & B-1. Also, GABA and Betaine are helpful. Herbs include: Ashwagandha, Bacopa, Fo-Ti, Ginsing, Macuna Purens, and Reishi Mushrooms. Further, the supplements Acetyl-L-Carnitine, Choline, DMAE, Methylcobalamine. Vinocenetine, and Trimetylglycine are high in TMG.

Ideally, you would monitor levels of the various above supplements with lab tests before and after. Barring that, never add more than one at a time and pay attention, especially, to mood swings and general wellness before adding the any new ones to the mix.

Also, have the charts done. You may find that your Sam E levels are high. High levels of any of these enzymes and fatty acids are a bad sign just as are low levels. It most likely means that bottle-necks that are causing problems.

HL MSM, Methylation, Epigentics, and More...

Dr. Andrew Rostenburg
https://www.youtube.com/watch?v=qqi7RHJvDvk (Red Mountain) reinforces the following things that I spoke of in

my previous book, including:

- How Alzheimer's is a doctor engineered disease caused by the low fat diet.
- How genetically engineered crops have profound effects on birth rates of mice.
- How we are genetically similar to fruit flies, but what is very different is how they are turned on and off genetically.
- What is normal?
- How nutritional deficiencies during pregnancy affect the entire life of the offspring.
- Methylation problems are about how we move carbon atoms.
- What is aging? How it works.
- Estrogens in diet are causing early periods, and they are present in health and beauty products.
- We are not living longer as we are told and lifespans have decreased from the 1800's.
- Green foods help us in more ways than we'll ever know.
- The problems caused by birth control pills.
- The adrenalin reward circuit. How we are creatures of habit.

Some new genetic & epigenetic ideas from him on this video:

- What is spinal bifida? A cleft palate is spinal bifida of the face.

- Alcohol causes problems in B-9 deficiency.
- Vitamins affect how you look.
- Autistic kids have marked facial features.
- Birth defects are the result of low or missing B-vitamins.
- So if, in uterine, you get enough methyl groups, it all generally works well.
- MTHFR mistakes increase miscarriages by 250%
- Most of the significant defects occur at or near fertilization.
- Deficient B-vitamins mean that you can't detox well.
- Autism today occurs in about 1 in 50 kids and is increasing.
- Mercury keeps you from detoxing.
- People most affected by chemicals don't detox well.
- B vitamins are numbered by when they were discovered.
- What we do affects the next four generations.
- Cool discussion about 23 & me testing.
- If you have the Apo E4 gene, it is a risk factor for Alzheimer's. In that population, a high fat diet may be a risk factor.
- Depression is often a problem with low methyl folates.

He gives you a very good explanation of 23 & me testing here and how to use the information (also why there are problems with it right now). Realize that this science is moving too fast to report. Search it before you do anything, but epigenetics will remain.

Universal Water Theory:
How it Applies to this Unified Science

Everyone agrees that water is essential to life, but few get the full picture as I theorize it here:

I experimented for maybe five years every day (and for virtually twelve hours a day) with water, quantum electrodynamics as it applied to water, and lab grown crystals and their relationship to water. This was a passion, as I attempted to understand how water affected: first, stacked stainless steel cells, then how the cells affected internal combustion engines.

The net effect of this work was what we now term the CrystalPack4U. It is a lab grown four crystal set that actually creates a slipstream around cars to the point that one can drive a car in a downpour without the need for wipers. But that is just the most obvious effect. It profoundly affects engine performance. Furthermore, in tuned down versions, they profoundly affect the vibratory rates of human bodies and these same rates are what separates a healthy human from diseases like cancer. Keep in mind that water is a liquid crystal and crystals both in our bodies and elsewhere communicate.

So these tuned crystals change the frequency of the cooling

water in an engine and the water (blood) and cellular surface crystals in your body where, as Dr. Lipton says, key information is exchanged.

Now listen to what Dan Nelson says on:
https://www.youtube.com/watch?v=xKZe81V0yOI

Dan's explanation of water is profound and some of this stems from his work, but much is from my own work and understanding. Please allow me to take it one step further:

Water must be present in every cell for a cell to function and also in the mitochondria (check out this incredible reference): http://www.nature.com/scitable/topicpage/mitochondria-14053590 The powerhouses of the cell that I discuss elsewhere are well described at the above link. Interestingly, when any animal dies, all of these mitochondria shut down and the conversation stops in unison. It is a light switch and no one knows why.

There is a vibratory conversation between all cells that is electromechanical (quantum electrodynamic) in nature (noted in our reference as an electron transport chain). All nutrients influence this and especially organic metals. When you eat a food, the nutrients are taken to the cells and the vibrations from it balance the vibrations. This balance occurs instantaneously in every cell in your body. In fact, I submit, it exceeds light speed.

So you may say, well, when I eat moringa leaf (as Ann M. does in the discussions below and moringa is just an example), you immediately report that you feel revitalized. That is, these moringa nutrient component vibrations, once they "soak in" (and digestion occurs from the mouth to the gut), are instantaneously carried by the water in your body to every cell. It is very much the same as turning on a light switch, just as death is the opposite. Therefore, the quality of the water that carries this nutrient is actually more important than the nutrient itself, but it all counts.

Also, all of the nutrients in moringa make up an orchestration of vibrations that total one (call it) sound. For this reason, you should never just take a single sound in any quantity or in one sitting. You always want the orchestra. Think of all foods as frequencies and water as the carrier. However, the water and cells are all a frequency. If you start out low, there is far too much work to do to raise it to the level that we are aiming for.

Water: an Analogy

Water is really far, far more complex than our minds can actually grasp. I offer the following:

In your body, think of water as the wiring in your house. If you go back to the days when electricity first came into use, house wiring was bare. This can be considered as the same system that most use today and that is, city water. It is treated with chlorine (a poison), but it serves us well as far as most understand.

We can use the bare system to run your house and some still do today. It will power a few light bulbs and simple appliances. With added load (stress) it becomes less efficient. It can be touched off and shorted, blow fuses, and even set the house on fire (kill you) under certain conditions.

Next, we have the additives that Dr. Patrick Flanagan, the brilliant and creative scientist, gave us some twenty-five years ago. These literally came from another planet. These include covered wires, but they incorporate resetable pull panels. They take away the fire hazard of the basic system of old. There are other ways of going about this, as he will tell you, but most never take the time to install them and the cost in personal effort is just too high.

Now, we have Dan's water. This system is fully programmed and automatic. It really does not rely on wiring at all and very little can ever go wrong when you use it. There are systems here that work unseen to the human eye. The electricity is literally transferred through the air as Tesla conceived it originally. This is God's way of making things happen. Since there is no chance of a short in this system, no fires occur. With this, you can leave this house unattended and visit others with the knowledge that you will always be safe. Plus, it will make your city water healthy.

Quantum Wellness: How It Ties In

First, watch this 2 ½ hour video:
https://www.youtube.com/watch?v=LFSRTsLOiv0
If you are not totally familiar with this astounding topic, this video should open your eyes. There are plenty more videos on this, but this one will teach you: First, that this is truly science; Second, that quantum science does not necessarily follow anything that you thought was true; Third, that it follows that what we once believed was reality, is not true. That is we can truly be in two or more places at once (the double slit experiment); Fourth, that time is flexible. Finally, water (and by extension, all materials can be altered by the human mind) as the minds of those involved move the pH as much as 1.4 points on the pH (power of hydrogen) scale.

So, with these simple, yet robust experiments, we now see why I stated in my first book that the human body is a quantum machine. At the cellular level, when we read some of today's most profound researchers (like Dr. Bruce Lipton), we begin to see why medical science with its roots in pharmaceutical drugs and pain management is bound to fall by the wayside as we begin these profound new ways of opening this wellspring of healing and antiaging. As a result,

I hold that the methylation pathways are actually less complex than they appear and can shift in ways that objective reasoning will not allow us to believe for the very reasons stated above. That is, our attitude can move a quantum outcome at the mitochondrial/ micro-level in ways that make no objective sense and this outcome will manifest at the objective cellular/ macro-level, thus short-circuiting objective medicine.

For these same reasons, certain key frequencies can alter outcomes in ways that were previously never predicted and healings based on various sound and light spectrums will occur that defy "science."

Videography explaining the above:

Listen to Dr. Tanya English explain the basics of Quantum (microcellular) Healing at:
https://www.youtube.com/watch?v=government-nXTIE4 XQ
Dr. English is a Chiropractor who has learned the subtle nuances of this ultimate healing methodology that can defy space and time limitations.

And the following interviews with Dr. David Hamilton, Biochemist. Placebos work:
https://www.youtube.com/watch?v=iDywixw8N18
Here Hamilton, a PhD scientist, tells us that his experiences in

the pharmaceutical industry led him to learn that self-healing (placebos) far exceeded the healing rates of drugs with all of their downsides.

Quantum Entanglement:
https://www.youtube.com/watch?v=AtahXDuU4So
The very basic premises of the science and how it defies the logic of Newton.

The Science of Belief:
https://www.youtube.com/watch?v=qBB4bfkkAho
Beliefs affect everything at a much greater rate than ever previously thought and now we know why. Hamilton tells us that.

Dr. Bruce Lipton, Cellular Biologist and Rob Williams: Epigentics and How You Change Your Biology:
https://www.youtube.com/watch?v=VYYXq1Ox4sk
From his Dr. Lipton's talk

Biology of Belief... the direct biology of what English and Hamilton above, told us:

- Genes Do Not Control Anything.
- Genes are Blue Prints (Programs) of the Protein.
- Signals from the Environment Allow Cancer to Happen.
- Proteins Regulate Biology.
- Environmental Signals Activate Engineering Genes and

- Direct Mutations.
- Perceptions and Your Beliefs Control the signals and these Signals are Never Random.
- You Are Never a Victim (spiritually or biologically).
- Cancer Is Activated By The Nervous System.
- Cells Always Move Away From Toxins As a Means of Protection.
- Love is the Most Important Aspect of Environmental Protection.
- How Stress Shuts Off Immunity.
- When Beliefs are Wrong and Stress is High, Cells Make Mistakes.

The second half of the lecture:
Rob Williams, Psychologist, continues and teaches how to actually apply the above: Perceptions rewrite behavior... The Subconscious mind

- Perceptions are awareness.
- Experiences affect awareness.
- Beliefs are conclusions and these determine your biology.
- Facts are your subjective opinions dealing with Information and tools... affirmations do not work.
- The Subconscious mind is about long-term memory. It's about beliefs, values, and your biology... not the future.
- He explains muscle testing (dousing...which I use). It is a yes or no Subconscious communication system.
- The whole brain state... using both hemispheres at the

- same time.
- Everything is energy... As quantum physics teaches.
- Changing beliefs is instantaneous and all biochemical disorders can be changed in an instance (the opposite is also true).
- You need not know the cause of a disease or incorrect fixed pattern (an embedded subconscious belief) to change the effect (the disease or fixed pattern).
- Meditation is single focused. It does not work here despite what others teach.

https://www.youtube.com/watch?v=jjj0xVM4x1I

Online Discussions (titles in italics):

From this pont on, I give you Coconut Oil posts with my commentary based on various topics that relate, generally, to methylation therapies and this new "Unified Quantum Science."

One theme that is repeated here constantly is that in this new "Unified Science of Health," we simply never take large quantities of any supplement without good reason and how our subconscious wellness affects our overall health.

I start with Paul, the gentleman who first led me to this methylation sequencing science, who I am grateful to. Then, Harold, and next, Mark, who is interestingly a horse farmer who knows about HL MSM, as previously mentioned:

Dr. Any Yasko Genetic Panel Test

On 7/5/2014 11:14 AM, Paul [coconut_oil_open_forum] wrote:
> *This is exactly why I got Amy Yasko's genetic panel test*<

Oh... really nice chart:
http://www.heartfixer.com/AMRI-Nutrigenomics.htm

Dr. James Roberts
>
> From: "'Harold [coconut_oil_open_forum]" <coconut_oil_open_forum@yahoogroups.com>
> To: coconut_oil_open_forum@yahoogroups.com
> Sent: Saturday, July 5, 2014 11:01 AM
> Subject: [coconut_oil_open_forum] Possibility why some people have difficulty with MSM
>
> *Attn. Jim--It has to do with the Methyl Cycle. This was taken from Dr. James Roberts web site. He is from Ohio.*

> *http://www.heartfixer.com/AMRI-Nutrigenomics.htm*
>
> *"CBS initiates the trans-sulfuration pathway, converting homocysteine into cystathionine and its downstream metabolites. This is the most important Methyl Cycle defect and is present in 90% of the patients whom we have tested. We treat CBS (+) individuals with dietary animal protein and sulfate restriction and supplements designed to neutralize*

*ammonia and speed up clearance of sulfite/sulfate."
Laboratory findings consist of an elevated urine sulfate level, a low or, low normal, blood homocysteine level, an elevated or high normal blood ammonia level, and itive findings of ammonia, sulfite, or sulfite upon Asyra testing. My initial observation is that individuals with heavy metal burdens, upon provocative challenge testing, are likely to be CBS positive. CBS (+) individuals will be intolerant to sulfur containing drugs, nutritionals, and foodstuffs.*

> While sulfate is less toxic than is sulfite, it will stimulate the adrenergic (fight or flight) limb of the autonomic nervous system and stimulate a cortisol stress response, thus revving you up into an unrelenting biochemical overdrive. If you have a CBS defect, we need to restrict your sulfur intake, at least until your urine sulfate (and your body sulfate burden) has decreased. The amino acids methionine, taurine, and cysteine all contain sulfur; they are concentrated in animal protein (thus the restriction on animal protein intake). Many great nutritional supplements (MSM, N-acetyl cysteine, glutathione) that are good for most people, are a problem for you.
> CBS = Cystathionine Beta Synthase
> Hal

Very Nice and easy to comprehend discussion, Hal.

The Gut Factor/ Drugs

On 3/16/2014 2:54 PM, usndgh@yahoo.com wrote:

> *Please Jim, advise on the issue of indetermine colitis.*
> *Any advice on pre and flora probiotic, am currently on SULFALAZINE.*
> *I bought VITALACTIC B (L.plantarum and L.acidophilus)*
> *Please I will be grateful for any advice*

HI USNDGH:

The digestive tract benefits from pre and probiotics are well, known and widely accepted by many mainstream doctors and, by now, all naturopathic doctors. Therefore, telling you that proper gut flora is a path to healing, is not a leap. Realize that I am not a professional. I just report on what I read and what I have found beneficial myself. However a quick check reveals that SULFALAZINE is an NAISD (drug).

Interestingly, it produces side effects that sound disturbingly like the problem that you are treating (UC). Loss of appetite, nausea or vomiting, and headache are common. Interestingly, also, no one claims that SULFALAZINE will cure the problem, ever, but it is used to decrease the "occurrence" of colitis. This is typical of drugs and why we avoid them generally. There are a couple of exceptions with drugs that we use here "off brand" such as Selgin which has some interesting anti-aging side affects.

The people here (myself included) believe that there are natural cures out there that can fix your problem if you search for them. Hopefully, Duncan can help you with this.

Kind Regards, HUuman

HL MSM... Reports... Side Effects...

These are the kind of reports that awakened my suspicion that much more was occurring than I ever dreamed of with HL MSM. There are several in my first book and, while some may put them aside as unscientific, note that "Side Effects" take on a positive meaning with these protocols.

Also, note that these healings are real and were unanticipated as I mentioned earlier. No one ever suspected for a minute, that HL MSM was anything but a joint and arthritis cure. But as the below reports combined with a cursory rundown of what is now being reported with tiny amounts suggests that we seeing what amounts to would seem to be a break though. Time will tell.

Mark... Horse MSM Always Best

On 5/11/2014 6:12 PM, Mark wrote:
> *Hi Jim.*
>
> *This may be funny, or sad, but:*
>> *LOL... then be sure to tell everyone in the group. Your knowledge will be valuable, I can assure you.*
> *I was in the yahoo MSM group as well as the DMSO one, and when I tried to* **mention that horse stuff is ALWAYS best,** *I got tossed out of both without so much as any warning.*

> *I've been careful to not mention that ever since then...*
>
> *Best Wishes.*
>
> *Mark*

Mark:
This is our real story that no one ever had gotten out to the masses before my book. These facts have taken me literally fifteen years to establish. The two Beck Groups also have heard all of this and most people accept it as fact.

Keep in touch. I am beginning a new book and I want you in it, OK? You are actually an "expert" at this point. We could go on TV interviews together my new friend!

You are going to love my story, Mark. Nearly everyone in the CCO group gets it by now, though. They also did not get the fact that more is better and there is virtually no such thing as too much MSM!!! Those who tried more just got well. This is our real story. These facts have taken me literally fifteen years to establish. We agree also that MSM for horses is the best grade possible.

Fibromyalgia

Hi All,

Yes, I am using Jim's protocol. Started a few months ago

after reading his online book and I've worked up to two tablespoons of pure MSM powder a day. I swish it and it's not as bad tasting as it was in the beginning. I have had fibromyalgia for many years and nothing worked to help me feel better except going on a low oxolate diet but there was still something missing. When I started the MSM protocol, I began to feel even better. I have more energy and my hair which was thinning is starting to come back and it's been only a few months! My face which was blotchy has cleared up to the point where I hardly need to wear make-up. I will continue with it and report occasionally on improvements as they occur. I also use organic coconut oil in cooking, in smoothies and on my skin and hair. It is a marvelous product, healthful and easy to use.

Hi Ann:

You are the first person with fibromyalgia (only) to report on it. As you are aware, I never expected such great results as these.

Kind Regards, HUuman

Getting Better Gradually

I received a 5# bucket of AniMed MSM about a week ago and am taking 2 TBLSPN/ per day now. I had a problem in my right hip/groin area in that I could not sit crossed-legged or do the butterfly stretch without great discomfort. I couldn't cross my right leg over my left to put my sock on either. Now, I've noticed that I have no pain when I do either the butterfly stretch or sit cross-legged and can put my sock on without any discomfort. It was just a gradual thing.

I haven't had any adverse reactions and was able to get to the 2 TBLSN within a couple of days. I think I'll stay at this dose for a couple of weeks then add another tablespoon. I think I was expecting some heavenly choir AH HA moment with this, but haven't had that. I guess all of my improvements will be just a quiet and gradual thing.

Virginia

Rates of Taking MSM

Hi All,

>Yes, I am using Jim's protocol. Started a few months ago after reading his online book and I've worked up to two tablespoons of pure MSM powder a day. <

From: coconut_oil_open_forum@yahoogroups.com [mailto:coconut_oil_open_forum@yahoogroups.com]
Sent: Monday, May 19, 2014 12:59 PM
To: coconut_oil_open_forum@yahoogroups.com
Subject: [coconut_oil_open_forum] Re: HL MSM protocol

*Jim has stated his opinion many times that two Tablespoons is really just the bare minimum to achieve any real results, so the reason your progress has been **so slow** is likely due to the small dose.*

Personally, I recommend that you ramp the dose up as quickly as possible *until* you get an adverse reaction, then back it down. Then I think you just night achieve that 'heavenly choir AHA moment'...

The only reason I can see to go so slow with this protocol is if you are someone who indeed has an adverse reaction a higher dose. The fact is that many people don't. E.g., I never had *any* (adverse) reaction, and I've taken as much as 10 Tablespoons in a day (spaced out an hour or so of course) over a few weeks, and many others I've talked to have had no bad reactions to much higher doses than yours either.

I'm getting the feeling that it is not all that common to have adverse reactions, maybe it only happens in those who have a really high toxic load, or maybe a combination of that and a badly functioning liver - there are lots of different factors that could figure into it.

But, obviously and by all means, stick with what you are comfortable with.

Of important here, is the length of time positive effects take to show up, regardless of the supplement taken. It seems that three months is an average span of time just to see the beginning of change. In the meantime expect the best and wait for the miracle.

Olushola

On Tue, May 20, 2014 at 10:44 PM, Peter [coconut_oil_open_forum] <coconut_oil_open_forum@yahoogroups.com > wrote:

New Zealand... Mesothelioma

Hi Jim and Group,

This seems like a good moment to touch base and update our situation. My hubby has mesothelioma. Both of us remain in very good health. We have now been taking MSM for over two years and continue to discover improvements in our health. On a conventional note, my husband's recent blood tests are all normal, including the liver profile, which wasn't so good when he was diagnosed two &1/2 years ago.
This, of course, is the only test we had as we continue to refuse x-rays and scans, much to the oncologist annoyance.

We also do not use the word "cure" but by optimizing our bodies we feel they are able to cope with and over time, we hope, make some real inroads into the disease.

Our protocol remains the same; we are having about 1 Tblsp

MSM a day-more if we feel the need, magnesium, astaxanthin, selenium, kefir with ground flaxseed, veggie juices, and have eliminated most flour and sugar from our diet. We have done a little recent reading on iodine Jim and wondered if you had an opinion on its possible benefits.

We also want to reiterate that we have eliminated all joint pain from our bodies and now after over two years feel an extra level of vitality has come back, reminiscent of our youth. The improvements seem to keep coming.

Also, following another discussion I saw, Hubby and I only use coconut oil as deodorant these days. It seems perfectly adequate. Best wishes to all.

Deanery

MSM is Not an Essential Food

Hi Lynn & all:

Do you eat seafood, Lynn? They are dense foods also. But no food type is absolutely necessary. Here are the basic thoughts that my book discusses on this topic:

The point in density is that you do not have to work as hard to extract the nutrient (vibratory) content... and it is all there. Duncan Crow and I agree that you just can't totally thrive on vegetables. Do you supplement the missing nutrients? Still, none of this is really necessary, read on:

I specially recommend Moringa Leaf and Hemp supplements if you are going to stay away from the dense (animal) foods. These offer the total package except for L-Carnitine. The goal is to eat as little food as possible and get the maximum extraction. It's simple. Realize that, as Dan Nelson teaches, it is the vibratory content of your food that keeps you alive. The rest is passed through and wasted and doing this takes a huge amount of energy. That is, extracting vibratory energy from food is a very expensive and energy wasting process. Below is the crux of what I wrote in my book that no one discusses. Most get to the HL MSM part and stop, but the real information is further on:

The three essential mineral vibrations most lacking in soil in developed countries are: Sulfur, Magnesium and Selenium. I recommend supplementing these, But most here are deficient in others as well. (And most plants can never provide all of them).

While what I say is esoteric and controversial, there are people who simply don't eat food. They absorb the vibrations from the ether... the quantum energy that Dan Nelson teaches. Most don't have a clue what I am talking about, but I have seen it work on cars with our CoilPack4U. It can run any machine, including your body on vibration. I have videos on You Tube showing it running full sized, 3000 lb cars on 150-200 mpg. It works!!!

And no, MSM is not essential to anyone's health. MSM is for people in this flawed world who are taking their nutrient vibrations from soil, a soil that is depleted and starved and that has been farmed using petroleum-based fertilizers for decades.

The fact is that those reading this have been starved of sulfur since they were born. They stole what their mothers had in the womb as a basis and that, combined with the little that they can get with green foods and marine life, will keep some of them healthy till about age 40, when the real trouble begins. In my case, it started at about age five and by age 26 I was in big trouble. Had I not discovered HL MSM, I would be long gone, as is my father.

The best evidence of what I am saying rests with the Dr. Stephanie Seneff/ Mercola interviews. She taught me most of what I know about MSM even though she knows nothing about it. Don't kid yourself, if you are over age 40, you are severely deficient in sulfur and you will die of it if you do nothing. The form of "disease" can be anything from heart failure to cancer, but it will happen and, for most, at the very young age of 80 or less.

So what is a natural life span? As I suggest in my book, and this is all theoretical now: I am pretty sure that we should live, as Dan Nelson suggests, like the ancients did in the bible... between 300 to 800 years. In fact, we probably should all die of accidents, not disease. The body is very good at keeping itself healthy if we provide it with the basic vibrations that sustain it. These vibrations are encompassed in the word love in all its meaning. If you spend a half hour a day in deep contemplation gathering up the love that I am discussing, you feed your body with these needed vibrations.

Kind Regards, HUuman

>>>>> On 5/25/2014 8:48 AM, Lynn [coconut_oil_open_forum] wrote:

>>>>>> *Just can't do it now. I know my body craves meat instinctually. The smell of my husband grilling hamburgers yesterday makes me drool. I wish I could choke down some humanely raised beef. It's akin to eating feces to me. That's how repulsive it is to me.*
>>>>>> *Except for the smell until I shake my head clear. Especially the smell of steak. It makes my body weak and my stomach churn. That's nature for you.*
>>>>>> *Lynn*

Purchasing MSM

>>>>> On 5/3/2014 10:28 AM, Katy Bryce - Clayworks wrote:
>>>>>> *Hello James,*
>>>>>> *I just got your book and am really enjoying reading it. Thanks for putting out such a great publication. I am from the UK and I have been looking for the AniMed horse MSM*

that you recommend online. It doesn't look like they supply it here in the UK. In your knowledge, am I generally safe taking another brand of horse MSM (or of the ones they have listed on Amazon UK)? Is their purity generally safe for human consumption?
>>>>>> I really appreciate any knowledge you have on this, and look forward to hearing from you.
>>>>>> Many, many thanks again.
>>>>>> Katy
>>>>>>
>>>>>> Katy Bryce - Director of ClayWorks
www.clay-works.com
01326 341 339   0778 978 0391

On 3 May 2014, at 19:24, Jim wrote:
Hi Kathy:

There are two things that you want: A fast-moving product is the real issue. Secondly, cheap products for horses and animals move quickly. It would never make sense to buy a product from the US if they make the same thing in England or some place closer. Realize that it is made from wood, so a country with a lot of trees is a good place to look. Purity, when the product is handled in bulk, is not generally an issue.

Just don't be misled by supplement companies selling small quantities and pushing how pure their product is. AniMed certainly has nothing special about it except that it meets this simple criteria. Personally, I can't even get the flakes down and they are the most expensive of all.

Please tell your friends about my book and thanks for the kind words.

Cheers, HUuman

It Grows on You

>Hi, Jim,

>Can't thank you enough for sending this updated version of the book! I'm looking forward to your next one, as well!

>My skeptical husband whose shoulder has been killing him for two months was finally willing to try my suggestion of MSM plus Great Lakes Collagen Powder. Within 36 hours he was begging me to keep the regimen up for him, sheepishly admitting that it had helped significantly!

>What amazing stuff!

>Cherwyn

Katy's Experience (Wow! Nice commentary on my 1st book)

On 6/2/2014 5:32 AM, Katy Bryce - Clayworks wrote:
> Begin forwarded message:
>> From: Katy Bryce - **Clayworks** <katy@clay-works.com

>
>> Date: 19 May 2014 12:34:04 GMT+01:00
>> To: Jim <huuman42@gmail.com >
>> Subject: Re: Horse MSM
>> *Hi Jim,*
>> *Thank you for your fantastic email and your answers to my questions. I am really enjoying reading your book - I have read many books on alternative health and yours is very down to earth and simple, as well as cutting edge, exciting and honest. I am looking forward to implementing many of your ideas and suggestions. As I read a book, I normally turn down a page when there is something interesting that I want to re-visit. I think most of the pages are currently turned down on your book at present! I am about to re-read it a second time!*
>> *I am now through the worst of the detox reactions, I hope, and am beginning to increase the amount of MSM I take daily - trying to get up to the larger amounts so that the sulphur can really start working on the joints. I am looking forward to the joint issues becoming a memory, as you say.*
>> *One thing I am very interested in is your Quantum Orange Creme and using DMSO and MSM as a transdermal way to get nutrients into the system whilst by-passing the tricky digestive system - is this something that you are producing on the open market that can be bought from you/a distributor? If so, where is it possible to purchase it? If not, would you be willing to share a recipe/method? Also, do you have some more info on the dissolving of vitamins/minerals in DMSO as a delivery system?*

>> I hope you don't mind answering my questions. I am just very intrigued and interested.
>> All the very best,
>> Katy

On 9 May 2014, at 16:24, Jim wrote:
>>> Hi Katy... **interspersed:**
>>> On 5/9/2014 4:52 AM, Katy Bryce - Clayworks wrote:
>>>> Hi Jim,
>>>> Many thanks for getting back to me and for the detailed advice on how to go about choosing the MSM. That all makes great sense.
>>>> I have a few other questions that have arisen as I am reading your book and hope you don't mind answering them:
>>>> 1. When you take up to half a cup per day, are you splitting up the doses throughout the day?.I have been only able to take one tablespoon at a time, otherwise I find that it doesn't dissolve in my mouth.

One heaping tablespoon is all that I ever recommended trying to swoosh at a time. That is a lot of swooshing! The only reason that I ever stopped at ½ cup/day was based on how much time we have in a day to take it. Life must go on and taking MSM could consume your days. However, you could perceivably continue taking it all day long and suffer no known harm. No one even knows if there is an upper limit. How much water would you have to drink before it harmed you? Well, MSM is less poisonous.

>>>> 2. Is there any benefit to taking it on an empty stomach

or around food? Or does it make any difference? **No difference.**

>>>> 3. I have been taking the MSM for about one week now and have been feeling pretty lousy - I am assuming this is the detox reactions? **Yes. Back off some.**

>>>> In your experience, should this abate soon?
Sure! (But not for everyone)

>>>> I am very willing to go through this if there is a brighter light on the other side.
No need to feel badly. But chances are that you do not have enough stored toxins to harm you seriously.

>>>> 4. How much whey protein do you normally take per day? i.e how much per day for it to start having a therapeutic effect? **A lot more than anyone you'll likely talk to. I do two heaping tablespns of Now Whey combined with a tablespn of multicolor Maca and a level tspn of moringa smoothed out with A-2 cream from our local farm. Just to give you some idea of how much that is, I drink three quarts of cream a week... wow! Most doctors would have me on their heart attack list. All that I have for breakfast is this mix.**

>>>> 5. I have taken the MSM crystals quite a lot in the past with not much result to see.
We know... (They do nothing in small quantities worth taking about).

>>>> I have mixed the crystals in water and drunk in the past. Is the main difference with your protocol the fact that you are keeping it in your mouth + the large amounts that you are taking?

Yes. I say in my (previous) book: If someone claimed that eating peas healed cancer and you came down with it, would you eat one pea per day? No. You would eat a normal serving at least.

>>>>Again, many thanks in advance for answering these questions. I am sure you get a lot of emails like this.

Fewer all the time Katy... but all are welcome. Most here are getting really sophisticated at this point like Julie's just the other day. Quantity and duality are easy. Systemic function is not so simple.

Thank you for your service to humanity. I will certainly tell others about your book. I know a few who will benefit greatly. I am trialling the protocol on myself first!

I am not hoping that you do not have massive joint problems like I did to prove this out, but even minor ones will taper off quickly enough and, guess what? Chances are that you will outlive everyone not on these protocols and remain in perfect heath till your time comes. No promises, but that is pretty good news, huh?

>>>> Have a great day and I hope there is a good game of tennis somewhere in the offing! I hope I am able to perform like you soon - I am 38 and unable to play 10 minutes of tennis right now without joint pain! That certainly is impressive.

Oh, you saved the "best" news (worst for you) for last. You my friend, will be astounded that this was ever true and, eventually, all pain memories will fade.

This is just how it works. Keep playing those ten minutes,

though, it moves the sulfur through your joints and keeps things moving. It is like greasing an old car... your joints quiet down and, finally, they work like new. Watch the Dr. Stephanie Seneff videos and read her news to see just how far this is going.
>>>> *All the very best,*
>>>> *Katy*

Ketogenic Diet... Diet Discussion

Talk on the Keytone Diet

<http://www.lewrockwell.com/2014/02/Joseph-mercola/slow-aging-to-a-crawl-and-shrink-your-waist/>
> on Feb 3, 2014 2:29 pm (PST) .

My Introduction:

If you really want to stay young, mean, and lean... even de-age a few years, read this and watch Dr. Attia's video.
Reading this, when done well, takes time if you follow the links, but it will add years to your life if you grasp the essentials... plus, it will help assure that your life is kept pain free, which makes it all well worthwhile.

The Ketone diet is not to be confused with raspberry ketones as Dr. Attia says. Dr. Attia, an oncologist, gives us a technical talk on his Ketogenic Diet which is basically the same as what I term the LCD.

However, his results will really never equal what I offer because I include these UWPI and HL MSM Protocols. With these three combined, you do not have to wait for the marketing of the Lab Ketones (that will be sold soon as Dr. Attia suggests). That is, they will never deliver the full protocol components.

"Cancer eats sugar" as we heard from Otto Warburg, the Nobel Prize winner of the 30's. However, while Attia is very careful in his mainstream answer, his explanation here on what cancer eat and why is nicely explained.
.

The CDC recently came out with an advisory that Admits this for the very first time what Attia is saying. However, this has been common knowledge among the insiders for many, many years. Nothing has really changed except that the American public consumes more sugar than ever and cancer rates have increased along with that rate. This is not to suggest that cancer is simply a dietary disease. It is far more complex than that, but sugar has been a big contributor.

Interesting that the Super Bowl half-time show in 2014 was sponsored by the sugar drink, Pepsi. That really struck me as weird, but no one generally gets it.

So we could say that everything in the four paragraphs below is also in agreement with the LCD, but for those who are not doctors, I am also sure that the average person will "get" what

I have to offer. Also, I give you added solutions that will guarantee that you are producing ketones without having to subject yourselves to lab equipment and blood samples as Dr. Attia did.

Dr. Attia misses in a few places as he is still hung up on cholesterol issues, avoids fruits and the correct animal fats with his focus here on ketones. I would say that he will do OK, but would improve if he discovered the entire program. < HUuman

What is this Ketogenic Diet?
In the words of Dr. Joseph Mercola:

> Dr. Attia consumed what is known as a ketogenic diet http://articles.mercola.com/sites/articles/archive/2013/06/16/ketogenic-diet-benefits.aspx that shifts your body's metabolic engine from burning carbohydrates to burning fats. Your cells have the metabolic flexibility to adapt from using glucose for fuel to using ketone bodies, which come from the breakdown of fats---hence the name "ketogenic." Another term for this is nutritional ketosis.

As an aside, many types of cancer cells do not have this adaptability and require glucose to thrive, which makes the ketogenic diet an effective therapy for combating cancer. http://articles.mercola.com/sites/articles/archive/2013/03/10/ketogenic-diet.aspx.

A ketogenic diet requires that 50 to 70 percent of your food intake come from beneficial fats. http://fitness.mercola.com/sites/fitness/archive/2012/08/10/fat-not-glucose.aspx such as coconut oil, grass-pastured butter, organic pastured eggs, avocado and raw nuts (raw pecans and macadamia nuts are particularly beneficial. One of the fastest ways to /prevent nutritional ketosis is by consuming sugar or refined carbohydrates.

Besides restricting carbs and limiting protein, you can also strengthen your ketone engine with intermittent fasting, which is what Dr. Attia did. He restricted his sugar intake to about five grams per day, which is quite extreme and much lower than I recommend for most people. He consumed a moderate amount of protein, and the rest of his foods, 80 percent of them, were fats.

But his approach, as radically as it was, really proves that a ketogenic diet can have profound health benefits, not to mention blowing the saturated fats. Dr. Mercola

My Goals as Opposed to Dr. Attia's

My Comments:

I talk about this at length in my first book, but basically I hold the OT Bible to be a conversational history book, but nevertheless, available information worth drawing from even though it is often poorly considered as a reference by scholars and even Christian churches. The common explanation is that, "Their years were different in those days." Has the earth's tilt changed in six thousand years? No, but what have changed are our water and the farming techniques which have leached organic sulfur from our diets as mentioned earlier.

My own goals include a long, disease-free and pain-free life, but I am already happy with what I have gotten so far and the rest is icing on the cake.

I am not interested in riding bikes across country, (leave that to Dennis), but I do enjoy being able to play tennis at the highest level that I ever have and I plan to improve ... and fully expect to. Why not? <HUuman

Dr. Mercola (who introduced Attia)

http://articles.mercola.com/sites/articles/archive/2011/09/01/enjoy-saturated-fats-theyre-good-for-you.aspx
> theory of heart disease out of the water, once again.

> Please note that I have recently revised my position on using low-Carb, long-term, and now believe that the low carb, low to moderate protein, high healthy fat diet is appropriate for most who are insulin or leptin resistant. Once that resistance resolves, then it likely becomes counterproductive to maintain a low-carb approach.

Once your weight, blood pressure, sugar, and cholesterol

normalize, you can increase your carbs. Personally, I now consume several pieces of fruit a day and have two dozen fruit trees in my yard, but my body weight, fat and insulin resistance are all optimized.

On Mercola's comments

My Comments:

Good to see that Mercola is getting on board with fruits. One can simply overdo the anti-carb thing and, especially, organic citrus fruits with their skins and lemons in particular, are high on my list of foods. The skins are very high in nutrients and, all told, if you eat a tree-ripened lemon with skin, you are consuming a nutrient bomb of outrageous proportions.

Just avoid the breads, the packaged foods, and the pasta and you will be good to go. <HUuman

On Lyme Disease...

On 5/25/2014 2:43 PM, Lynn [coconut_oil_open_forum] wrote:
> *I have heard the spirochete theory and read up on it. But spirochetes have been around in nature forever and it's because of our food, environment that makes us less resistant. That is my opinion. My husband says it's the government.*
> *The doctor that studied all the Lyme, CT people still*

practices in Mass. I think. Not far from me.
> Lynn
>
> On May 25, 2014, at 2:34 PM, "Lynn [coconut_oil_open_forum]" <coconut_oil_open_forum@yahoogroups.com> wrote:
>>
>> No...my husband refuses to research Lyme. Just doesn't want to be overwhelmed by the info and he depends strictly on his doctor.
>> So, I do all his research for him now and coordinate his treatment.
>> He has been rubbing CO on his "Bartonella rash" daily for months and it has receded. It basically is from Bart "blowing up" the blood vessels in my layman term. Basically, it's inflammation from its occupation of the red blood cells. It could be the CO or some supplements that reverse Bart he is on... Or a combo... Not sure.
>> Lynn
>>
>> On May 25, 2014, at 1:56 PM, "Jim huuman42@gmail.com [coconut_oil_open_forum]" <coconut_oil_open_forum@yahoogroups.com> wrote:

Hi Lynn:

Lyme is awful stuff. Has he researched it on the web? Realize that it sprang up not far from a government research lab in

Lyme, CT and was never known previously. Have him to watch the You Tube videos on it and read the many articles that appear when you Google it. Certainly, no one is going to tell you that it is a man-made disease, but it is possible. My friend Rich, who studies with Dan Nelson (search him), can treat it effectively.

Our bodies (and I start out with this in my book) are Quantum Machines. < HUuman

Vibrations in Diets

>>> On 5/25/2014 10:28 AM, Lynn [coconut_oil_open_forum] wrote:
>>>> *Hi Jim...That is an interesting post to say the least!*
>>>> *No, I don't eat seafood. Just a random bite of a scallop here and there if I lost a bet. (People can be cruel...lol)*
>>>> *I take Hemp capsules and will get some of the Moringa Leaf. I started taking Hemp to "oil up my knee."*
>>>> *I am a newbie to supplements, but am learning a lot.*
>>>> *Yes... I tell my husband with Lyme and co-infections that he could get hit by a bus any day before the lyme gets him. Though we protect his body as much as we can.*
>>>> *I had clinked the coil link u posted before, and I thought... cars? Lol.*
>>>> *My goal was to avoid a plica surgery.*
>>>> *Now my goal is to maybe just to be able to recover from it.*

>>>> *I have an appt with a third orth who isn't as scalp happy. I know u are not a doctor, but if it was you... would u have the surgery? Hypothetically speaking?*
>>>> *Lynn*

See MSM is not an essential Food for the answer to this, above.

Beyond MTHFR

On 7/7/2014 5:13 PM, jeannettechilds@yahoo.com [coconut_oil_open_forum] wrote:
>
> *Excellent explanation on Methylation, Estrogen Metabolism, & Gall Bladder in this presentation and how they all tie together.*
>
> *Estrogen, Choline and the Gallbladder*
>
> *image*

Hi Jeanette:

Thanks for this as we listen to the few experts out there at this point with expertise in these very specific areas. I believe that these pieces are just too complex for any one person to ever get it all.

What is important to us is how these various genetic pathways interact with body chemistry to teach us where we may supplement... such as Acetyl-L-Choline, Taurine, and 5-methyl folate that naturopaths have been discussing for years.

"It's the Liver Stupid," the title, came to me when I read about problems like these.

Note Taurine is a great supplement (and cheap), but MSM is cheaper and it delivers organic sulfur in spades and it is the primary nutrient in virtually everyone speaking of these methylation cycles. Beyond that, of course, the two methyl groups in MSM are the inside linemen that allow this down field run.

Yes, we need experts like this one, but you have protocols that he has never heard with plenty of evidence that they do these things.

Kind Regards, HUuman

>
http://beyondmthfr.com/2014/05/11/estrogen-choline-and-the-gallbladder/

> Estrogen, Choline and the Gallbladder

> Ever wonder why so many people are getting their gallbladder surgically removed? What is causing all these gallbladders to fail? Listen to Dr. Rost . . .
> View on beyondmthfr.com
> Preview by Yahoo
>Hi Mike & Marsha:

>On 7/17/2014 6:56 AM, ege [coconut_oil_open_forum] wrote:

>Hi Alobar and Jim,

>Thank you for your replies. I'll try the small amount+swish until it deadens your taste buds+lots of water plan. I've been an old but silent member of that forum back from the days when Duncan was an active part of the conversations - and I was 27 :)

>So I've also followed quite a while his low carb+whey protein+selenium protocol. The results were so amazing even for a slim person as I am. And now, I'm all ears about MSM and other >important -and usually neglected supplements. My miracle ingredient is definitely an ACV by the way, and I drink it regularly. I also stick to low-carb eating as much as I can, stay active and >also grateful for what I am and have.

>I've learnt so much from this forum and I appreciate all the input.

>*Thank you for being there and providing us with lots of fresh ideas!*

>*Cheers from Istanbul,*
Ege

My Comment: Ege had problems with taking HL MSM and wrote later to the group. We got some very good advice in response. Also, as I say later, he is just not old enough to need the high levels of MSM that I discuss, but they certainly will do no harm unless he happens to be CBS +/+.

Drinking Ice Water

On 7/6/2014 7:44 PM, islandsky [coconut_oil_open_forum] wrote:
>
> *Do Eskimos ever get sick? Makes me wonder. Mike*
>
> ----- Original Message -----
> From: 'Marsha' [coconut_oil_open_forum]
> To: coconut_oil_open_forum@yahoogroups.com
> Sent: Sunday, July 06, 2014 4:51 PM
> Subject: RE: [coconut_oil_open_forum] Recipe Share
>
> *I just have to comment on this. I have drunk nothing but icy water my whole life, the colder & icier the better, it's been 30+ years since I've had a cold or sinus infection. Same as Alobar, I perspire and don't have any elimination problems. I*

have not been sick, period, thanks be to God alone. Marsha

Do Eskimos even drink ice water?

If they did, how would you know?

First, how old are you and how long do you plan to live? No single influence is likely to determine that and you know it. The average puny lifespan in the US is now, what? 78 for men? My intention is to multiply that but a factor of eight or ten. If you are interested, you will not keep this train of thought that you are suggesting. Old, repeated mistakes are not going to help, ever.

Some people smoke cigarettes and live to be over a hundred. And that proves what? Most all people eat sugar, consume carbs at a high rate, and never do the protocols that I suggest. A very select few drink enough water (even tap) to keep them from dying at age 90. Finally, the primary reason that ever your maintain health is, as epigentics tells us: Your attitude is the game changer, not ice water.

Dan Nelson (a Christian) and I believe, that the OT stories about people living hundreds of years are absolutely correct. My suggestion (I am not preaching and I am not here to change your religion), is that God does not care a wit about how long you live. Why? Because you will come back and relive this story till you finally learn the higher love that God entails and It is timeless.

Yes, this is called reincarnation... a notion that Christianity gave up at the Council of Nicea in 325 AD, This was the date that the Romans took control of the Church. In my estimation, most of the spirituality was lost in the Church as the Gnostic ideas were thrown out of the scripture. I also do not see the bible as infallible, but I also see it as reasonably correct and, in general, a wonderful book. Along these lines, I see the NT as two books (as do many biblical historians), the Gnostic book, John, and the others that changed as they were repeated and passed on through word of mouth. The Books of John still suggests reincarnation, but many of its gnostic ideas were eliminated.

Modern day Christians are quick to explain that the OT scriptures were using a different yearly system than today's when they read about Methuselah. I say, hogwash. Years passed at almost exactly the same rate 10,000 years ago as they do today and people knew how to count. In fact, they were probably quicker mentally than we are today. However, as Dan says, the water has changed in its life-giving content and is now no longer sustainable in terms of longevity. He claims to have proven this as a Quantum Scientist and I accept his explanations.

Kind Regards, HUuman

HL MSM Results (a conversation between old guys)

On 7/9/2014 10:36 AM, Christopher

[coconut_oil_open_forum] wrote:
> *Jim*
>
> *Thank you for your support.*

> *I am halfway through your book (thank you very much) and I am now at three tblspn MSM per day, I started slowly in February.* **I have some form of arthritis in my wrists and it seems to me that there is improvement there. Another thing is that I was becoming incontinent prior to starting with MSM, I recently turned 70, and now that problem is over with, thank goodness, and it can hardly be anything else that has changed that.**
> *Being now well established on LCHF I want for nothing. My morning coffee contains both butter and coconut oil and my meals are similar to my new friends habits which he posts here: http://www.eatlowcarbhighfat.com/ you can read his story in English here: http://www.tommytappar.se/?page_id=143*
>
> *Thanks again*
> */Chris*

Hi Chris:

Great news. But at three tablespoons/day, I am at a loss as to why you still have a sign of any arthritis at this point, but the Lord acts in strange ways, LOL. It will come soon enough. Please post when it does. Everything helps.

I can hardly recall how long it took to get rid of my juvenile hip arthritis (my worst of many forms), but it was probably two years. Most joint problems are well on their way out within two months, but obviously we have a stubborn case.

Incontinent? I hate the idea. Fortunately, I discovered HL MSM before it all got started, so I avoided even the thought. Did you notice that we are contemporaries? I assume also that, if you are married, your wife is crazy about you (or just can't keep up)? My friends are always saying how their sex drives are pretty well gone and I say... oh sure... right... Ha!

Have you noticed also that you are more mentally alert and just feel better about life? It is harder to evaluate, but the fact is that at these high levels of methylation, it has to occur. Mental illness in all of its forms probably just slips away with HL MSM... especially with all of the other things that we have recently discovered.

Yes, my coffee is loaded with fats too... and I always drank it black after my Air Force days. Now it's sooo groovy with gobs of fats... cream... yum! Have you tried my whey/cream/moringa prior to coffee? I almost live for that creamy stuff and coconut oil would also be welcome there.

I am thinking that you might be a great candidate for the 2086 reunion my friend... interested? We'll need some really old farts there to show off our high level of wellness. Do you play tennis?

Tommy is very cool... please have him read my book! I want that guy as a spokesman. Get him onto Methylation, HL MSM, and Whey.

Kind Regards, HUuman

Nutrition...the Staff of Life *(not Magnets)*

As you probably know, there are commercial magnetic (and copper) wraps for tennis players and runners now and I am sure that they all offer some relief. But I have to ask, why go through all of that when you need not have any joint problems, ever?

This is just one burden that I no longer deal with and I am happy to be past. None of these devices that you discuss will totally heal you and the reason that most of us ever have joint problems in the first place is quite simply, nutritional, even though trauma may have set if off. I have not had a single joint injury in fifteen years, while I was plagued with them for the previous 25 and was born with hip arthritis that even kept me from driving at age 26.

Recently, I have been trying to get my book to pro tennis and NBA players so that they can extend their careers another, say, ten years. That would mean millions in lost earnings for someone like Maria Sherapova or Sarena Williams, both of whom are nearing the end of their ropes. Most pros are forced to quit because their joints are so stressed and fail more frequently. I know that HL MSM will fix that easily with no downside. These pros just master their games, then must quit because their joints fail. This is ludicrous and unnecessary.

There was a time when all of my fingers were racked with arthritis just as your pinky probably is Lyn. I would not be able to hold a wrench on a cold day. Now I know why and it had nothing to do with a lack of magnets (nor drugs), That, I can guarantee you.

The fundamental physical reason that we all age and become ill is nutritional, not magnetic. Keep that in mind. But it really is about frequency (all nutrients are frequencies), so magnetics counts to some degree. If you don't nourish the joints properly, it does not matter how they are vibrated or aligned. Exercise and vibration help deliver the food to the joint, but that is where it must end (but there is actually plenty more to this story as Dan Nelson will tell you).

Kind Regards, HUuman

Moringa Leaf... Powerful Nutrient!

On 7/11/2014 10:52 AM, Ann [coconut_oil_open_forum] wrote:

> *Hi Jim,*
>
> *> I got some Moringa Leaf Powder a couple of days ago and*

you weren't kidding - it's like a shot in the arm. It's helping my energy levels better than any vitamins I've taken. It must be very bioavailable to the body. The only thing is, I'm not sure how much to take. The package just says four gm. per serving, but gives no guidelines as to min. or max. intake. How much of it do you take daily? If you have a moment, plus, give me the benefit of your advice.
>
> *Thanks,*
> *Ann M.*

Hi Ann:

LOL... if you can take four gm at a time, you are one tough lady, Ann. I am good for a level tspn max and sometimes that will give me diarrhea... when it does, it is Katy bar the door! No waiting. So, please, I know it is great stuff, but do not even try to take too much at a sitting. Start small and work it out. I was not warned and got a huge lesson.

I do a tspn of it two to three times a day. That will pretty much take care of your green food needs. A pound of it lasts me two months.

I also find it to be a great spice for smoothies... very tasty in small amounts with other stuff like cream and whey. However you use it, do not heat it above 140 deg F except as cooking spice... which it works well as.

Obviously, there is no minimum amount and I wish that I could get more in, but the body says no.

This is no doubt the most powerful green food on this planet and it is used all over the world by people who have little or no access to these wonderful nutrients. It started in India, but is grown in Africa and South America and in poor soils. Every part of the tree is edible and it grows at an alarming rate... like 4" per day. It will grow annually in temperate regions, so you can raise it yourself in summer.

My friend in West Africa has a tree growing in her yard, so it is everywhere and it has become a great cash crop for them. These third-world countries are using this for its nutrients and also exporting lots of it.

Kind Regards, HUuman

I agree, Lyn. And virtually any fermented food is a good choice, it means that we are getting the nutrients that are predigested by bacteria, but without the sugar (they ate it).

Salt is a powerful nutrient that is full of minerals and it is great transdermally, also. A swim in the ocean is nutritionally beneficial. We gravitate to things that are good for us.

A sun bath is good for us and we should get ½ hr per day, every day, but current medicine says that it causes cancer. Unless you overdo it, we now know that it helps keep you cancer-free, think of the sun as a nutrient: Too much of any nutrient is bad for you. No SPF please... it blocks the good vitamin D and negates the value. Astaxanthin is a great sun protectorant. If you happen to overdo your stay, it will jump in and keep you from peeling, plus, it has many other benefits for skin health.

So real self-education is the key. Listen to the guys who are paying attention, not the idiots who are taught fifty year-old wives tales in nutrition. No matter what your papers read, you can be either. The internet is alive and well and we have access to intelligent MD's who are actually paying attention like those on the Vitamin C Council.

So we have always given cows a salt lick, but doctors have said that salt causes high blood pressure... and they are right when they are discussing processed salt. So just remember, no processed foods ever and you avoid the issue.

Kind Regards, HUuman

Buying Moringa Leaf

On 7/12/2014 8:35 AM, 'Taffy[coconut_oil_open_forum] wrote:
> *Please, would you share where/whom you bought the product from?*

> *Thanks,*

> *Taffy*

I have bought Moringa Leaf from at least four different places and I have never seen a lick of difference in quality or taste. Native Pharm, Organic India, Shamans Mrkt, and Vitacast

I go for price now... but make sure it comes in an aluminum resealable package as these do.

Kind Regards, HUuman

Vibratory Healing Techniques

Lab Crystals

On 7/12/2014 6:26 AM, 'Ryszard [coconut_oil_open_forum] wrote:

The crystals are to be used in four packs and on Cars, about four feet from people, Lyn. We store hundreds of them in a room in stacks. You would never want to sleep in that room... in fact, you probably could not.

Most agree that they enjoy the feeling of having them on their cars (and no one has ever complained about them). When used as they are designed to be used, they have allowed us up to 150 mpg (at a steady 50 MPH over two miles of level road)

and double the rated power on a dyno test. I have video documentation of cars doing just this on my website.

When programmed for people's health they must be used at much lower frequencies and not continuously. We do not sell them for this, but the would be very effective therapy and, likely, more effective than magnetics (it is about frequency and power).

As others posted here, the gauss ratings (power/ force) on magnets just don't normally cut it and I agree. Commonly, they are a very weak method of what we are doing. However, if they work for you, fine. It tells me that your problems were likely minimal (or was it that you healed yourself as any of us can do). In fact, you are far more powerful than these crystals that I am using on these cars.

Finally, there is a vast difference between buying a therapy from someone else and one that I have developed on my own over about five years, agreed?

This scares you? Well, I guess it should if you do not understand it. I have a very good idea, by this time, of what I am doing. We have spent about $200,000 on this technology and it works really well, but people just do not believe that it works, so it is difficult to sell.

I know from my experience with our Lab crystals that orientation is everything and I have not heard anything here about it. If I point the crystal in the wrong direction, it will produce negative effects. I am certain enough that magnets work in very much the same way.

Duncan Crow had a wand that he was excited about several years ago... same thing. This may all seem simple, but this frequency manipulation is far from simple. There are people like my friend Rich, who are super sensitive and can feel what you need and immediately know when things are not flowing properly.

The bottom line, though, is that I think that you are messing with some very high energy concepts even with magnets that can cause as many problems as they can fix (about 50% of the time, actually, if you place them incorrectly). Magnets may not carry the energy of our lab crystals, but they are strong enough to cause problems in the wrong hands, IMHO.

Kind Regards, HUuman

Magnets

On 7/11/2014 9:56 PM,[coconut_oil_open_forum] wrote:
>
> *What I am "messing with" has healed me over and over and over. Peter has made his magnets as fool-proof as he possibly could. They are color coded and touch coded.>*

> *The only time Peter's magnets create problems is when they*

are used wrong. That is why I started out of the gate with recommending the complete Wellness Kit; so you get the book that gives the education to use them correctly. If someone does not know what they are doing, yes, there is a huge chance they will use them wrong.
>
> Even Peter finds them flipped sometimes, but that actually doesn't cause him problems. He said he gets hyped up like he had ten cups of coffee. But when I would find any backwards, I would get strong allergy symptoms. This was easiest for me to detect after I had begun to consistently have more clear days than allergy days. When I was sick every day or most every day, I did not see that pattern. But I learned right away to check my placement all through the day and especially if the sniffles and watery eyes would start out of the blue when I was otherwise clear. That kind of stuff just happens. But then when the wrong ones are righted, there would be quick resolution to the wrong energy supply and my symptoms would weaken or disappear altogether.

> Lyn

The key phrase here is "Correctly Placed."

I doubt that anyone (here) knows what that really means, but Peter might.

> Magnets, rightly placed over an organ, will definitely improve the function of that organ. I have been using the

Supers from Peter's Wellness Kit on my liver to cure allergies that I developed a few weeks after starting to work in a warehouse in Nov. 2013. Symptoms were awful by the time I went onto Peter's yahoo group in January to asked for help. I was very sick, both there and at home. But I knew without any doubt, to take the avenue of magnets to have the best results at a turnaround.
>
> I knew some of the magnet positions already for what I wanted to do. That is, to boost my immune system and aid my body to detoxify. But someone on the group told me allergies are a liver problem, so I put one super onto my liver. Then someone told me to reposition the belt I wore with the super and other magnets; that it was too low if I wore them on a belt. So I googled a picture of the liver and saw how big it is and decided two supers were in order. I then moved the belt up to the bottom of my rib cage. Once I did that, the symptoms I was having right then disappeared within minutes. I knew I was on the right track then.
>
> I did more than liver regen for this, tho. I also wore magnets from the WK in a pattern that boosted my immune system, wearing some over my spleen, and kidneys. Then I wore still others to help my body detox at night. Then Peter gave me a heads-up to wear the detox pattern during the day, too, and that helped me a lot. I have worn these day and night from about January, to mid June. Those are three methods of treatment that can be used singly or in combination like I did. The detox method is great by itself to help improve sleep. I

have also flushed excess fluid using the detox treatment by itself. This also helps build up the immune system as your body detoxes at night.
>
> It took about a month to start seeing small changes to the pattern of symptoms, but I knew to just keep at it. (Me and magnets have quite a history in these 5 years.) The situation I was trying to reverse was a severe level of assault on my immune system while staying in that dust-mite infested place from 4 to 6 days a week, putting in from 40 to 64 hrs a week. Plus, my body was seriously stressed at the start of work because it had been over 5 years since my last desk job employment, and then the job I jump right into is the fulfillment warehouse of a nationwide major dept store. There were a lot of adjustments to figure out about myself in the first 8 weeks of their peak season. There was intensity within me and intensity at my job and my body just was not accustomed to it. I ate like a team of horses and could get enough fluids into me. When I had a day off, I slept 12 hours easily and still was not real rested. One day I went to bed at 5 pm and slept right through to my alarm at 4:30. In addition, the job was very dirty (amazing how dirty plastic-wrapped items are!) requiring us all to wash our hands twice each time to get them clean. Then the soap was very drying on our skin. I had to figure that all out and then the allergies hit.
>
> I still wear them, tho not every day. And not all of them at once except on work days. On my off days, I might only wear the daytime/nighttime detox and the liver regen. Or I will wear

the sternum placement and the liver regen. Whichever I want to treat, but always coupled with my liver regen. But I can let them all off more often now.
>
> *I am so glad I did not have to do what all the others who get allergies from there do--drugs.*
>
> *So who is Dr. Arthur and how does he/she know about magnets?*
>
> *Lyn*

More on Magnets (and related science):

On 7/10/2014 9:45 PM, Joe[coconut_oil_open_forum] wrote:
>
> *Dr. Arthur said the magnet would remove the acidity from my liver, and viruse-like acid, so it would remove viruses from my liver and supposedly improve liver function quite a bit.*
>
> *Joe R*

This is a very interesting thread and I thank Lynn for starting it. Please allow me to shift it a bit as we discuss a related topic dear to my heart.

So what are you doing when you are using magnets? They obviously affect iron, but not most nutrients and most likely not genes or proteins. Iron, of course, has some profound effects on heath. Excess iron has been linked to heart disease, especially in men, but it is generally considered a problematic, yet necessary, nutrient. By using a magnet on a daily basis, since there is iron (blood) everywhere in the body, you are aligning cells in the direction of the magnet and, to some degree, breaking up the coagulation of blood.

The liver, as you suggest, may be improved by them in some and we just do not know how they affect our vibratory rates, which are really the key to all organic function. The liver is the center of blood production (and just about everything else along the way, which is why the title of my book, "It's the Liver Stupid") and blood contains lots of iron. As the heart pumps blood, a magnet will affect it. Why it would be better to align all of these cells is about anyone's guess except as it pertains to blood sticking together as I suggest.

I have physically seen how a computerized, charged lab crystal can align water molecules on my car windshield and I sell them, called CoilPack4U, online. Obviously, they have profound effects on the human body. On the car, they cause the fuel to be aligned and increase the car's power and mileage far more than any magnet ever could.

We had been trying magnets for decades if not centuries and never has a magnet come close to what I am suggesting here. An altered crystal, then, will have profound alignment effects on blood cells and break up any that want to stick together. But these are far more. They literally change the field around your body in ways that science can't measure. What other effects they may have are left to the imagination, but they are profound, for certain.

If you wore a CoilPack4U (they are pretty big 8" by 3" in diameter) around your neck, I can guarantee you that you would see much more profound effects than with any magnet that you could even lift up, let alone wear. There is just no comparison in the power of the two. This is quantum energy and it is simply incomprehensible to anyone who has observed its effects. Others mostly blow it off as impossible.

Magnetics and gravity are also quantum effects in themselves. Science today has all kinds of false notions about these two forces and only a few cutting edge pioneers have a real clue as to what they are doing. Watch the "Through the Wormhole with Morgan Freeman" show called "Gravity" to get a whiff of what I am suggesting. The CoilPack4U is a step beyond both that virtually no one is even looking at currently.

Also, too much of a good thing can be bad. When we are working around (building) the CoilPack4U's, we have to take frequent breaks because we just get too juiced up after about an hour or so. Some people can't stand to even be around a stack of them where we store them. After a several hours of close proximity, we just start shaking as if we were on a chemical stimulant like methamphetamine. However, we have also been told of some remarkable healings from those who drive with them. Finally, if you have a CoilPack4U on your car, I can guarantee you that you will never go to sleep at the wheel and you will never need windshield wipers again, LOL.

How this quantum energy ties into methylation and epigenetics, I am not yet sure, but I can guarantee you that this is all closely related. That is, these crystals affect your outlook positively and that is what epigenetics is all about. Do magnets too? Maybe, but nothing like what I am suggesting here.

Kind Regards, HUuman

> On 7/10/2014 8:32 PM, mk [coconut_oil_open_forum] wrote:
>>
>> I have shared this before, but know very well that often news gets lost and forgotten. So I will share this again.
>>
>> *The mysterious world of magnets came into my life about 5 years ago. Since then, and having bought a set and learned more about them and using them over and over for lots of different things, they have completely changed my life and how I fight this battle for health. I have used them for structural pain issues, (back, foot, finger) and for internal health issues (immune system boost, liver regeneration.) They have helped and healed without fail in every single instance where I have put them to the test. I cannot urge anyone enough to get a set of Peter Kulish's bio magnets and do the same. His website for the bio mags is biomagscience.net. The place to start is with*

the Wellness Kit, which comes with Peter's book that tells you why they work, how to use them, and what to use them for. There is about nothing that magnets cannot help. In one man's case that Peter shared on his yahoo group, they put a paraplegic from a motorcycle accident back on his feet and onto his motorcycle with complete control and healing. Twenty doctors told this patient that he would never walk again.
>>
>> *The body naturally wants to heal. But sometimes it can't because of some abuse that is in the way of healing. We are electric beings. I know someone who can make a lightbulb glow when she holds it. We respond to power and thereby create power. When we are sick or injured, that power flow is seriously hindered or even stopped altogether. Magnets work by being that power source that jump-starts your body's own natural abilities to heal. Wear the magnets until the sought relief is attained, and then continue to wear them after for a few more days. It's that simple. What's more is magnets don't make you stink. :-)*
>>
>> *His gas saver magnets work, too. I saved a lot of money this last winter.*
>>
>> *Everyone should have magnets in their arsenal of health weapons. I completely and totally believe in them.*
>>
>> *Get onto his magnetictherapy today from yahoo group and you will have an automatic membership discount for anything on his websites. You will also get in on any and all sales he*

runs through the year.
>>
>> Be well, Mk

On 7/11/2014 12:47 PM, mk[coconut_oil_open_forum] wrote:
>
> >>*think I had something like that done on me... <<*
>
> *Jane, you lost me. Magnets are not something you can just go to someone, get a treatment from and leave. At least that is not my experience. Is that what you refer to in your brief comment?*
>
> *Sometimes magnets are a quick treatment; but the quickest I have experienced is an hour. Tho, I believe it was a vastly different case. It was a case of a sore pinky finger from work. I basically "lift weights" all day long as I restock merchandise in that huge warehouse. We have to make our numbers, so I would take a lazy man's load of merchandise out of a box at once whenever possible so as minimize the number of times reaching in for the items to restock the shelf bin box. My hands were very sore and I cleared all of the pain with reflexology. All except that pinky.*
>
> *So one day I put two magnets on my hand--one on top (the positive side of the magnet), one underneath (the negative side of the other magnet), and the pain left in a short while. I had that joint loosened up from all the reflexology I had been doing, so the magnets could go right to work moving that*

lymph out. But most times magnets take constant wearing for a couple days, and in my most recent case this time of use, for months to right my system to take that daily assault.
>
> *Peter's Wellness Kit will make a believer out of you.*

Beck Devices

On 7/12/2014 10:15 AM, Joe [coconut_oil_open_forum] wrote:
>
> *What I had was a Sota Silver Pulser, I may even still have it. I'd put a wrist band on and adjust the output so I'd feel an electric shock on my wrist and it supposedly killed all viruses in my blood stream every 15 minutes or something like that. I just never noticed it making me feel any better. I'm sure it was working right.*
>
> *The CS I always made with distilled water and never salted-- the last thing I wanted was to turn blue.*
>
> *A few years ago, August an 87 man, failed to yield and turned in front of me on my 21 speed bike. We had the green light and was doing about 30 MPH behind some cars. I broke my left ankle and my lower leg became infected and I was scared it would turn into OsteoMyelitis (infected bone). I took antibiotics for a few days, but didn't want to. I asked for advice on a website and actually used urine soaked bandages to cleanse the wound and gradually, the infection went away.*

That was a rough time for me. On crutches, one day I noticed the infection and how the wound actually smelled like rotting meat. I went straight to the ER, and had a cab get me there...on crutches... Not fun. It took me 4-6 weeks to finally heal that wound. It was about the size of a half dollar coin where the car bumper hit my lower leg. When it finally closed up, I felt relieved. That was the slowest healing wound I ever had.
>
> Joe

Hi Joe:

Properly used, the Beck Sota devices have proven their worth, Joe. The device may have been working correctly, but you may not have been using it the right way. Also, invaders simply may not have been your real problem and killing them could make you feel worse. Die-off causes stress just as with the HL MSM.

There are two Yahoo online groups dedicated to them and one led me to this CCO Group some years ago... via Duncan Crow. Again, as with magnets, these things are dangerous when not done correctly, but they are far more likely to produce positive results because they simply have a lot more force behind them. I cured my dog of a cancerous tumor once using one, so they do work.

Kind Regards, Huuman

DMSO

Using DMSO as a Joint Rub

On 7/10/2014 10:14 AM, Jayne[coconut_oil_open_forum] wrote:
> ps - put this on my hip also . . .
>
> I could use some other things, like Absorbine, Jr., but chase people out of the house with it
> or use a Stop Pain spray with menthol in it! That is stinky too . . .
>
> Jayne
>

Hi Jayne:

Sure Jayne... Make sure that your hip is clean (no lipstick or hairspray on it and that your hands are free of soap or detergent (lots of water helps). Then puts some drops of DMSO on your hip. This is a killer external treatment for all joint problems, just as is HL MSM orally is internally (unless you happen to be one of the few who is genetically prone to organic sulfur/over-methylation).

I am not really sure what Absorbine Jr is (mostly menthol to kill pain), but I can guarantee you that it will not actually cure you of anything. Nor will any Stop Pain Spray with the levels of sulfur that it has. Use the two above sulfurs.

Whey Protein Isolates will help too. These are the structural foundations that keep you alive. Your problem is caused, most likely, by a lack of organic sulfur in your diet... and you are delivering it to your hip in two different ways. It just has to get better with these two treatments.

Don't be confused, be well my friend. Eat your greens, get plenty of animal fats, take your methyl B supps, your D-3 (or get ½ hr of noonday sun every day), and enjoy yourself in every way possible. This is your life. It's going to be a lot more fun without pain. Plus, interestingly enough, you are just going to feel better in every way.

Kind Regards, HUuman

DMSO Externally

On 7/9/2014 9:35 PM, Jayne[coconut_oil_open_forum] wrote:
> *THANKS Jim -*
>
> *life, yes, for sure :-)*
>
> *I use an oil which I rub on knees, neck and where needed - it was assembled by a nurse - has Olive oil in it, DMSO, lavender oil, etc.*

Hi Jayne:

I make my own spray DMSO after shower spray and creams. First, magnesium oil that I spray on after shower that has some DMSO, then rub down with something similar to yours, but be careful please.

The concern is to never use a DMSO based product unless you are totally free of all things that you do not want in your blood, because it will go there. The same with any mixes. You must ask the question, do I really want lavender oil in my blood? I would say no and never include the two... separately, sure.

The point is that DMSO is about as serious a chemical is there is on earth in that it does just what it promises. My cream is comprised of mainly supplements like: magnesium, astaxanthin, B-12, B-6, B-1, D-3, C... that I am very certain will not affect me negatively. You say "etc." And that is the big question.

So when you use a DMSO cream/oil/spray, think: Would I inject that with a syringe? If you would have any concerns, just don't use it. DMSO is wonderful, but brainless. It does not care and it passes all body defense barriers immediately. Hence, my warning. This is you telling your intelligent body: You are getting this even if it is bad for you. So like it or lump it!

Kind Regards, HUuman

DMSO Myths

On 7/11/2014 7:26 PM, Melly [coconut_oil_open_forum] wrote:

> *With DMSO, do I want the other drugs that would come with it in my brain. I take the DMSO with colloidal silver.*

Hi Melly:

DMSO is not a drug and it does not contain any (within it)... seems someone has led you astray or I am not understanding your comment. DMSO is quite simply two methyl groups and an organic sulfur group with noting else... or Dimethylsulfide.

DMSO comprised of these two very important organic chemicals, and absolutely nothing more, is identical to MSM except that it is not yet oxidized. So it is very reactive. When ingested or used transdermally, it becomes MSM as it becomes oxidized... thus, Dimethylsulfoxide (or methyl sulfonyl methane which is abbreviated MSM for us earthlings).

Interestingly both DMSO and MSM can shift back and forth between the two (gain and give up the oxygen) and, thus, reinvent themselves. They, once ingested, then, become the same chemicals. This makes them magical organic chemicals that no others can duplicate once ingested. I always have suggested taking MSM because it is just easier to work with orally.

Using it with Colloidal silver should not be an issue and the two should work better together (according to what you are attempting to accomplish) as long as you take the proper precautions. Again, consider that you are you are basically injecting colloidal silver into the tissue when it is used with DMSO.

Kind Regards, Huuman

Himalayan Salt

On 7/11/2014 2:24 AM, mk[coconut_oil_open_forum] wrote:
>
> >>I still have not given up salt. Should I back off this habit<<

No, absolutely not. You are on the right track using Himalayan Salt. Our bodies are made of salt and water. So it is essential to replenish the body with not just water every day, but salt. Just be sure it's a salt with color and you are fine.

On 7/11/2014 Lyn [coconut_oil_open_forum] wrote

>I, too, had fallen for this mainstream belief that we should use/ eat salt. But as I was learning this subject in the realm of REAL EDUCATION about what foods to eat, and started with Himalayan salt, my body actually craved that salt. It was a different kind of crave sensation, too. It was more like a yearning inside, making me reach for that salt shaker each time I plated my food. It was like I had starved my body of the

right salt all my life, but when I finally put a good salt into my diet, my body was immensely grateful. This happened repeatedly for days once I began using it. So now I use a lot of salt, all the time.
>
> *I also use Braggs Aminos. This is a fermented food and is helpful to you in many ways. So don't stop using that.*
>
> *If you have a Big Lots nearby, check through their food section. I have picked up grey salt there*
>
> *Lyn*

On 7/11/2014 6:14 PM, mk[coconut_oil_open_forum] wrote:
>>
> *I began using CS to fight this battle by taking a dose in the morning and using some in a nasal spray with essential oils that I used whenever I had symptoms. My use of the nasal spray has gotten less and less as I cleared up and got less and less symptoms. I want to keep using it, tho, so this week I started to try to remember to spray my nose before bed, but I*

forgot a few days, not being in the habit yet. I don't have symptoms anymore, but it seems like there was still a little congestion up high near my eyes one morning this week.

> Friday, July 11, 2014 6:01 PM
>>What about damaged nerves for hearing and vision and a stroke as far as magnets go?<<
>
> Hi Mike
>
> I have my book in my lap and I looked up stroke. The book contains two references to nerve damage. The first one is not for anything in the head but it says to place the magnets above the injury. That doesn't really help me think of how you would use them to regenerate nerves in the head. But when I looked up the second reference for nerve regeneration, he recommends the Meridian Energizing Treatment along with Vitamin A, C, E, minerals and a Medical Nutritionist. He recommends doing this therapy for 2-6 months.

> To know more, I recommend going onto his website and

read and then call him. He knows far, far more than I could ever explain on here.
>
> Lyn

Vit C Discussions

Organic Vitamin C (Lipo C) has been linked extensively to MSM by many healthcare professionals as a powerful cofactor.

The discussions here are generally with regard to taking it separately and in high amounts and, of course, this violates the basic promise of this, "The Unified Science of Health." Here, we begin to see the mind set of these otherwise open minded people as they defend mega dose Ascorbic acid, http://en.wikipedia.org/wiki/Vitamin_C_megadosage
There are no winners and no one arguing here has ever taken a genome test to see what vitamins they should be increasing or decreasing.

Note that the final word here from Joe is that Lemons "get the job done correctly" and I predict that you will be hearing this more and more as time goes on and this new Unified Science opens the eyes of everyone on all of the now three sides of the medical community.

So we begin the debate:

> On Monday, July 14, 2014 4:17 PM, "Alobar [coconut_oil_open_forum]" <coconut_oil_open_forum@yahoogroups.com > wrote:
>
> *I don't have a link handy, but Eskimos get their vitamin C from raw caribou leg marrow.*
>
> *Humans are genetically flawed in that we do not make our own vitamin C. If we made it, we would make over 5 grams a day when healthy. Normally, that is what I take. When sick, we need much more. Too Much C and we get the runs.*
>
> *During a serous flu about a decade ago I took about 50*

grams a day for 3 days, then dropped my daily intake down to ~15 grams a day. People I knew went to the hospital and lost more than 2-3 weeks of work I lost only 4 days.
>
> Mononucleosis can be cured in less than 48 hours with saturation levels of vitamin C.
> http://www.doctoryourself.com/mono.html
> When had mono back in the 1970s, I was out of commission for over 3 weeks.
>
> Doctor Klenner routinely cured polio with mega dosing IV vitamin C during the 1948 polio epidemic.
> http://www.doctoryourself.com/klennerbio.html
>
> C needs to be taken throughout the day, not in just 1 or 2 doses.
>
> Seems to me it would be impossible to get 5 grams of C eating lemons, or any other fruits
>
> Some people contend that Ascorbic acid is but one

component of vitamin C. I think that is bunk. Carnivorous animals who make their own C, do not make or eat bioflavanoids. Linus Pauling (who received a Nobel Prize for his work on Vitamin C) agrees.
>
> Alobar

(Alobar's post corresponds favorably to the beginning Wiki reference if you check it out. Certainly, he is not going out on a limb here, it is just contrary to this new methylation science).

On 7/15/2014 2:37 PM, Alobar fellow moderator coconut_oil_open_forum] wrote:
>
> *Lemons are nutrient rich, but no substitute for vitamin C (High Dose ascorbic acid). C cures polio, mono, and a list of other problems. I have never heard of lemons curing polio. Doc Saul's website is my vitamin bible.*
> *http://www.doctoryourself.com/index.html*
> *Counter-theories are just speculation, IMO. It has been*

speculated that the reason not all sailors got scurvy in the days before lymies and krauts is that some humans are able to make their own C. Not proof, but no counter speculations I have seen.

> *Alobar*

On 7/15/2014 3:40 PM, Joe[coconut_oil_open_forum] wrote:

> *I agree with Alobar. Some of us have conditions that require more than just food sources of nutrients. This is when a nutrient acts to provide therapeutic levels of nutrients to reverse or control disease.*

> *I now take megadose Vit C with Biomagnetic therapy. The magnets enhance the action of Vit >C and have been very good at improving Hep C. With things like Hep C, we need to pick our >"poison." In a perfect world, yeah, lemons would be enough.*
>
> *> I don't know if VC cures Hep C, but with BioMagnetic*

Therapy it can detox and improve the liver so much that Hep C would be much less significant.

> Joe

The Germ Theory Does Not Hold Water... No High Dose Vitamins Please

On 7/15/2014 6:26 AM, Jim[coconut_oil_open_forum] wrote:

Then you agree with me Joe. That is my point: Nutrients are never independent cures. They always act in tandem to create their full effect. When you use C (or any vitamin) in a megadose and alone, you are basically using it like a drug, not a supplement.

I have never spoken against supplementation and take piles of them every day... But also I take plenty of variety and never megadose. These methylation tests give us reason to pile on certain ones according to the defective gene and that makes sense. Otherwise, I believe that you are creating problems.

By the way, how do you know what your magnets do with C? Just curious.

So, when you take megadoses of C, you get 7 to 14% and the rest goes down the drain by my references. When you eat an organic lemon, you get almost everything in it... the phytonutrients help you absorb almost all of it. Given this, if I were to take C (ascorbic acid), I would say that the most effective help in using it would come from organic lemon peel, not magnets. Just a guess... I really have no idea how magnets figure in.

This has nothing to do with what C cures or does not cure. I never discussed any of that, really. What I am disputing here is how you are using it (high doses alone). And how you get it (no cofactors). I believe that high dose C (or any vitamin) is a huge shock to your system and not good for most (there may be exceptions). That is what I got out of it in my own experience with it. It was not keeping me well and it was sometimes making me feel badly, so I gave it up years ago.

While I do recommend two tablespoons of MSM per day (or more), when you think about it, that is not so much given that it is a food. If you ate that many beans, it would not be considered a lot... and that was also always part of my argument. I also do not use MSM or even Whey alone. The whole idea is variety and cofactors.

Lipo C puts back a segment of what you lose when you do high dose C, but even that is not nearly up to what full spectrum organic lemons deliver. While organic lemons are not enough to sustain life and lack some essentials they are a bomb worth blasting. Only Moringa and Hemp can do that in the plant family.

Eskimos can probably just live on caribou, since caribou eat plenty of grass, but variety really is the correct spice when it comes to nutrition.

Kind Regards, HUuman

Hi Alobar:

This is only a theory that humans are "flawed" as I am sure you must be aware.

I believe that there is a reason for the "genetic Defect" that we are just not onto yet. The rest world is genetically flawed in the MTHFR gene stream except West Africans and even they have no way to produce C. Does that give you a clue?

I also don't except the premise that just taking ascorbic acid provides the same amount of available C (or even close) as the organic C in lemons even though it is accepted as so by most of today's alternative world and you as true.

What I am suggesting is that the cofactors in a lemon (for instance) make the C much more bioavailable. Therefore, despite what you read and think, you are not getting what you are counting. So Linus Pauling and I disagree and always will. Since he is dead, I doubt that I will ever win this debate.

Furthermore, since I missed zero days that decade ago, I must have done as well with no C supplementation. I have not had

the flu in probably twenty years and no colds since I started taking D3 maybe five years ago. I believe that colds are the result of not getting enough sun, not a virus as commonly believed (and Pauling accepted). In fact, I disagree with the entire virus, bacteria theory in principle and believe that they have it all wrong. It is really a case of nutrient deficiency (and poisons), not viral bacterial attack that allows disease to occur... per "**Antoine Bechamp**:"
http://www.247wereport.com/health-reports/item/152-honoring-Antoine-b%C3%A9champ-the-gentle-giant-of-science-medicine.html

The peel of a lemon is said to be as much as 100x as powerful as the flesh. I guess it is about who is counting, but lemons have a lot more going for them that just C. They balance out out your pH like nothing else and provide phytonutrients at a level uncommon to any foods. I really doubt that we have the science to even approximate their healing power at this time.

Kind Regards, Huuman

Vitamin C

On 7/14/2014 5:25 PM, Jayne [coconut_oil_open_forum] wrote:

> Is that an ever bearing lemon tree???
> They do exist here in Florida - I never knew that!!

> Jayne

More on C

This was from Bill Sardi (healthcare reporter). I have been in contact with Bill over the last twenty years and he always answers my emails. I recommend his newsletter:

According to one self-proclaimed authority, vitamin C therapy is nothing but health quackery. [Quackwatch.com] WebMD advises physicians that supplemental vitamin C is only marginally able to reduce symptoms and duration of the common cold. But the primary study referred to employed just

200 milligrams of vitamin C, barely enough to marginally raise blood levels of this essential vitamin. [WebMD June 20, 2012]

None of this negative science discouraged laboratory researchers in China, however. They inoculated mice with influenza virus and then injected 3 milligrams of vitamin C per gram of body weight. (Laboratory rats weigh about 300-500 grams.) [University of Wisconsin] So these animals were injected with 900-1500 mg vitamin C.

A 70-kilogram (154-lb) human weighs in at 70,000 grams. So the amount of vitamin C the lab rats received was equivalent to 21,000 mg in a human weighing 154-lb (70 kilogram). That is a lot of vitamin C. Far lower doses of vitamin C can be used in humans to achieve maximal blood concentrations.

So what happened to the intentionally sickened mice? Well, the viral levels in their blood were 10-100 fold lower than untreated mice. The vitamin C-treated mice exhibited very little lung inflammation, which in turn lowered their death rate.

[Chinese journal of tuberculosis and respiratory diseases May, 2014]

So how does this animal lab research translate to humans? Carol Johnston, a long-time vitamin C researcher at Arizona State University took a small group of seemingly healthy non-smoking men (tobacco reduces vitamin C blood levels) whose vitamin C blood levels ranged from adequate to low and gave them 1000 mg of vitamin C/day for 8 weeks. Over that time 11 of the men who took an inactive placebo tablet and 7 men who took vitamin C develop cold symptoms, a 45% difference. Duration of cold symptoms declined -3.2 days in the vitamin C-treated group. Another bonus: the males in the vitamin C-treated group were more physically active (+39.6%).

By the way, I stopped taking C as a supplement some years ago and now eat plenty of organic citrus peel, especially lemon, which contains gobs of organic C, but so do grapefruit and oranges, to a lessor degree.

Kind Regards, HUuman

Organic Lemons & C

Hi Alobar:

Where did I call C a drug? I said that you are using it "Like a Drug." I also said, "When you take any vitamin supplement in high quantity, isolated, you are using it like a drug." I wrote a whole book on nutrients to take along with my HL MSM just for that reason. While I may discuss it alone, that is never my intent.

There really is no such thing as a "protocol," period, but I do use the term. We are all so very different that no single level of anything is correct for all. That is why I say, "Start small, work up, and see how you feel." I also don't believe that I need to defend this advice. Show me where you think I am wrong. Now we know that genetic defects can make both HL MSM and Whey virtually poisons, in effect.

I take two quarts of heavy cream a week. Is that a good thing for someone with gallbladder problems? Not likely, but it works for me.

Like I said, I doubt that science is up to this level yet. But there may be some references. I have read plenty of "experts" who agree with me on organic lemons, but you need not be one to discover their magic. My first book discusses lemons at length in the group discussions, by the way. Lemon peels are a bit past what my book discusses, but there is some good science behind them in their high nutritional value.

Kind Regards, HUuman

On 7/15/2014 11:19 PM, Alobar [coconut_oil_open_forum] wrote:
> Lemons have much lower C these days than before selective breeding made them sweeter.
> I have never heard that ascorbic acid is mostly not used by the body. Got references?
> You call high level C a drug rather than a vitamin. I never saw that distinction anywhere. I side with Orthomolecular Medicine foundation. C does cure and prevent Scurvy. But you have to give high doses to get the full benefit. High C is medicine, not drug.
> Co-factors be damned! Research on C was done on Ascorbic Acid, not co-factors. Bioflavanoids, etc. are indeed

beneficial, but not because they allow more C into one's cells.

> Alobar

On 7/18/2014 2:31 PM, Tanstaafl [coconut_oil_open_forum] wrote:
>
> I challenge you to point to any single isolated 'vitamin' (like ascorbic acid) that has a longer track record (safety and efficacy), even when used at very high levels. This is debatable, of course, and there can be no winner.

Not even MSM has such a track record.

Agree... More below.

> There are simply no downsides to taking large doses of ascorbic acid, and there are very well know, scientifically proven benefits. And the anecdotal evidence far outweighs all of that.

There were downsides for me, at least, so I must disagree, in addition to the above arguments.

> I'm not knocking MSM, just getting tired of your knocking

ascorbic acid, pretending that it isn't as safe and effective - backed by real science as it is.

The real science has just taken a new leap that the above arguments are staunchly disregarding (The point of this book).
>
> On 7/18/2014 2:24 PM, Jim huuman42@gmail.com wrote:

Maybe, but that is not the point. The claim may be just as antiquated as the idea that you can remove all cofactors and not have repercussions.
> >
> > On 7/17/2014 5:09 PM, Tanstaafl [coconut_oil_open_forum] wrote:
> >>
> >> On 7/15/2014 11:19 PM, Alobar Alobar@Gmail.com wrote:
> >>> *"Co-factors be damned! Research on C was done on Ascorbic Acid, not some gobbledegook of C + co-factors. Bioflavanoids, etc. are indeed beneficial, but not because they*

allow more C into one's cells." Agree 100%. Some people try to claim that ascorbic acid is not 'vitamin C', but the fact is, ascorbic acid is what was discovered and defined.
> >> As 'vitamin C', by Albert Szent-Györgyi in the 30's.

This is not my argument or concern... More below.

> >> Yes, there are 'co-factors that may be related to ascorbic acid, but that is all they are only co-factors.

Only Cofactors?

The MSM Vs. Acerbic Acid Track Records

Hi Tans:

"HL MSM has no track record outside this CCO group to speak of." In one to three gram/day amounts, MSM has been tested about as much as you could probably expect testing on anything that has no possibility of making money for drugs companies. From most of what I have read small amounts are

a failure at joint repair... and I agree with mainstream reports that in one gram amounts, it is no better than Glucosamine (which is pretty good if you 'could' take two tablespoons of it without gastric distress), but better than Chondroitin.

However, I am not knocking C, for sure, and this is not a contest. This discussion is about cofactors and megadoses.

With all due respect, what I am knocking is where you are taking this. That is, that, apparently, everyone in this group should just drop plenty of C down their throats and it will make them all well in all of these lab-tested ways, without problems. This, just because Linus Pauling (who died of cancer, by the way), said so.

Pauling was an interesting guy in his era... a time when everyone was certain that mainstream meds were the answers to all of our problems. I respected his counter intuitive ideas, but now I am pretty sure that he was, while taking a step in the right direction, not correct. Yes, nutrition is the answer, but you don't just load up with some vitamin, all by itself, and ask everyone else to follow. I have never suggested this for any nutrient certainly not MSM.

I take plenty of C, probably well above 20 x recommended levels. I have for ten years or more. However, never would I take it without cofactors. While there has been some speculation that fruits contained much higher levels of C thousands of years ago... how do you prove that?

Certainly, we can easily prove that veggies have much higher levels of organic sulfur prior to cooking. Also, it's proven that they had far higher levels prior to how we are currently raising them. Dr. Seneff goes into this in detail. It may not be on the tips of all nutritional experts, but it can easily be shown. So, with that alone, taking as much organic sulfur as some veggie that you might consume at dinner makes perfect sense... flavors aside.

The methylation factors, the revolutionary story behind this, of MSM are still not really tested, but the results from so many are astounding. Show me, after all of these years, just one case where a person taking HL C got over mesothelioma, please. If they did, why did it not work for the founder-in- chief, Pauling?

Given what Paul, here, brought to the table, I have to believe that we are on the verge of an enormous find here that far exceeds anything I could have ever anticipated. It is coming and you, my friend, can be a part of it. I can guarantee you that everything that you ever say about HL C is not going to change anything. It has been said already. It made the news in the '60's, Pauling died, and it is going nowhere. Some like Alobar get good results from it and fine. I am glad for him and you.

The fact is that, actually, I never anticipated anything but soft tissue repair with HL MSM. I am totally blown away by what we are hearing. Since no one else previously ever did either, this becomes even more of a find. There is no placebo effect without prior knowledge, agreed? It is mentally based.

I am not buying that all varieties of lemons today contain more sugar and less C, just for the record. It may be true for some. These are trees... they last quite some time and there are probably hundreds of varieties and even wild lemons all over the world.

Lipo C... High Dose IV C
Hi Joe:

I would do the last, as you know. Any other choice is about taking someone's word for it. You and I are not doing any personal studies that carry scientific weight.

IV C, especially Lipo C, has seemed to perform well in some studies... but there are obvious downsides. Also, Lipo C is not cheap.

Kind Regards, HUuman

On 7/17/2014 9:00 AM, Joe R cubbycat51@charter.net [coconut_oil_open_forum] wrote:
>

> Peter Kulish the BioMagnetic author recommends megadose Vit C. He claims it can eradicate Hep C when used with Magnet therapy. He and Tom Levy MD work together. Tom Levy MD is also an author and has used IV Vit C to supposedly clear people of Hep C.
>
> Peter asked me "which do you want to do first?" in reference to my going after Hep C with Magnetism and megadose C, or by taking WF VC to balance my minerals via HTMA (as if the two therapies cannot be merged).
>
> I have to wonder if 750-1000 mg of WF VC [whole food vitamin C] would be more effective when used with Biomagnetism therapy than mega dosing Sodium Ascorbate Vit C with Biomagnetism therapy.
>
> Joe

The Bottom Line on the C discussion:

On 7/16/2014 1:02 PM, Joe [coconut_oil_open_forum] wrote:

This from our friends at the Yahoo Magnesium forum (from Joe):

As you can see, they too are right on topic of the current thinking on Vit C.

1) No amount of chemical ascorbic acid could equate to a small amount of whole food vitamin C.

2) Ascorbic acid does not, I repeat, does not have antioxidant properties in vivo (in the body). It has antioxidant properties in a petri dish, but not in the body.

*3) Journal of Medicinal Food
Volume 4, No. 4, 2001*
http://gbn.grownbynature.com/vitccholesterol.pdf

We found no in-vivo antioxidant effect with a 1,000 mg. dose of Vitamin C (acerbic acid) alone, but a significant effect with the combination of Vitamin C (ascorbic acid) and a concentrated flavonoid-containing Citrus Extract (Re-Natured® Vitamin C).

> On 7/15/2014 11:19 PM, Alobar wrote:
> > I have never heard that pure C is mostly not used by the body. Got references?

> Personally, I believe that it is only the excess that is not used.

> If you utilize the 'bowel tolerance' method to determine how much to use, and stay below it, then most of it is used by the body. Wish there was a similar tool to measure the effective tolerance (to determine the optimal dose) of MSM.

To your tolerance level comments:

Since there is no known tolerance level for MSM, it has often been expressed by many experts in testing it that it is less poisonous than water. So you need no single measure. The optimal dose is not important unless you are dirt-poor and can't afford to pay an extra few cents a day for more. For the small percentage of genetically defective people who can't take the extra methylation or sulfur, any level is too much. (read Dr. James Roberts p35 herein).

Obviously, C is not analogous to MSM. C creates all manner of problems at high levels. So there is no comparison.

Below are three (long) online references that refute Ascorbic acid as a vitamin C source:
http://www.thesynergycompany.com/v/articles_vitc2.html
http://www.radiantlifecatalog.com/whats_wrong_with_ascorbic_acid
http://www.thedoctorwithin.com/vitaminc/ascorbic-acid-is-not-vitamin-c/

On 7/27/2014 4:54 PM, Alobar [coconut_oil_open_forum] wrote:
> I'd be willing to bet that camu berry powder and whole lemons contain only minuscule amounts of C. I have no interest in daily doses under 5 grams. I won't eat GM corn, but I am not fearful of pure ascorbic acid, no matter where it is derive from.
> Alobar

Your interest should not be in how much C (or any other vitamin) contains... and you know this Alobar. Even by your system, it is about "Net delivered amount" (the golden rule of supplementation). This was, till now, how much can you actually get into your system. Now, it is more complex, but amounts still count.

Camu camu (also spelled kamu kamu) berry is good stuff, but it's 120 mg per capsule... I am thinking not as good as half a lemon with skin, but cheaper and easier to buy and take (and appears to stop the negative effects of cigarette smoking).

Lemon skin, never discussed, is said to be as high as 100x that of the meat. Organic lemon with skin is a powerful nutrient.

Try this: Take ascorbic acid at your "tolerance rate." Think about how you feel. Wait five hours. Then eat an organic lemon with peel and compare. What I suggest really counts is the actual results and this is no longer considered a numbers game, just as calories have little to do with weight loss. Listen to what your body says, not what your brain is dictating.

Those that I follow believe that the delivered C in 5 grams is probably around 500mg (@10%). What is actually bioavailable for use is anyone's guess at this point, but most of the guys that I would believe are saying: effectively, as Joe reported above, it is zero. Your numbers game tells us 10 lemons (w/o skin) per day to equal your ascorbic acid.

However, the Linus Puling Institute still sees no difference... This by two different human studies and the 1993 PubMed **http://www.ncbi.nlm.nih.gov/pubmed/8505665?dopt=Abstract** report agrees. Most agree that this study is quite flawed as is this one:
http://www.ncbi.nlm.nih.gov/pubmed/8302486?dopt=Abstract also 1993.

This 2013 study begins to ferret out the differences: **http://www.ncbi.nlm.nih.gov/pubmed/24169506** However, we are in a new era as this book points out. Your numbers game is no longer the bottom line.

I suggest that with the list of videos herein on methylation, your ideas will begin to melt... Methylation and Quantum Science set a new bar.

Nevertheless, we all like numbers and for C, these are what I see as about average:

The organic C delivered in oranges @ 69.7 mg vs lemons @80 mg, varies a good deal with product, but the skin is never included and oranges are bigger. Organic red grapefruit stands at C 79.1 mg, limes at 19.5mg, & Kiwi 64 mg. If high C numbers are your interest, Black Currents at 202.7 per cup win. Anyone can and will eat an organic tree ripened lemon, but not a cup of black currents.

We have always known that the real nutrient content of all fruits is concentrated in the outer skin. This holds true especially with C.
Camu, Camu, being a berry would include eating its skin.

But please, never eat skins unless you know that they are organically grown. The chemicals used with citrus trees are very high and they dye them for looks.

Transdermal Healing
and the Concerns it Teaches

On 7/14/2014 9:13 AM, Joe R cubbycat
[coconut_oil_open_forum] wrote:
>
> *(NaturalNews) More effective than oral supplements in many situations, topical application of nutrients is often an overlooked (although superior) method of delivery. Whether using magnesium oil for debilitating arthritis, iodine to heal skin cancer or water soluble vitamins for general health,*

topical creams, gels, oils and sprays are one of the best ways to receive vitamins and minerals that are crucial for healthy well-being.

> *The dilemma with tablets and pills. For those with a compromised digestive tract or failing health, metabolizing vitamins and minerals orally can be fraught with difficulties. Between digestive upset, poor utilization and the aggravation of yeast and bacterial issues in the gut, supplements taken internally, can be problematic. An alternative lies with a transdermal mode of delivery.*
>
> As observed by Mark Sircus, Ac., OMD in the article, "The Principles and Practices of Transdermal Therapy:"
>
> *"Traditional methods of administering medicine such as tablets or capsules get watered down and become much less effective due to stomach acids and digestive enzymes, before they eventually get into the bloodstream. Bypassing the stomach and liver means a much greater percentage of the active ingredient goes straight into the bloodstream where it's needed. In many cases, transdermal methods are used to help avoid potential side effects such as stomach upset or drowsiness. The full potential for transdermal medicine has not been explored by modern medicine though it has been practiced for thousands of years in hot springs around the world."*
>
> *Even when the system is strong, only 10 - 20 percent of*

standard oral vitamins and minerals are metabolized. However, these same nutrients have a much higher rate (up to 60 percent) when applied to the skin.
>
> Learn more: http://www.naturalnews.com/041695_transdermal_nutrients_vitamins_nutrient_absorption.html##ixzz37RqiLD6h

Hi Joe:

This is great advice and right on topic Joe... thanks.

It also serves as a warning as to just how powerful transdermal applications are and why we must be so very careful as to what we apply to our faces and bodies. Few really understand this... our own FDA, obviously, has no clue and they allow all manner of garbage to enter the market while exercising extreme caution... too extreme, in many cases, when it comes to oral supplements.

Please, always pay attention to what you put on your skin. It rejects virtually nothing adsorptive in nature.

Methyl B's Could Do Harm

Hi Paul:

Always good to hear from you Paul... & Yes. As you suggest, Joe needs a good wholistic doctor to help him evaluate his tests.

Still, given what I have read, for the vast majority of those without the funds or lacking the drive, I doubt that organic B's are going do anything but help. Agreed?

Joe with a high copper level or those with high lithium levels would not be expressed all that often from what I am getting. The point so often made is go slowly and pay attention. That always made way too much sense even before this sophisticated testing was available. I always said, add one supplement at a time & pay attention as practice.

On 7/16/2014 10:22 AM,[coconut_oil_open_forum] wrote:
> *after doing the 23 and me test you need to run it thru mthfr support to get the data...you don't get as much as u use to...but still helpful. This is the best: test:*
http://www.holisticheal.com/health-tests/nutrigenomic-testing
> *just got my results and will see my Dr. to go over them....so many factors...and a few meth supplements could be doing more harm then good... if lithium levels are high, you cannot take b-12, for example.*

Which Whey?

Hi Keith:

Take some time and read the protocol as Duncan Crow laid it

out from his study of the Uncial Program. It is very specific in what it does and his qualifications for the whey.

The protocol is not specifically about "getting quality Protein." We are really interested in raising glutathione levels and the wonderful advantages thus provided.

Now we know, thanks to the genetic testing, that all people do not benefit from adding whey or MSM to their diets. Some actually suffer from too high a level of methylation and they become ill when given organic sulfur, but they are a very small portion of the population. So these protocols are not for everyone, but they are generally very useful for most people and will keep you well and young... nice!!!

If you study the methylation pathways, what jumps out at you are three things: glutathione, organic sulfur and, of course, methyl groups (which mean $CHO3$'s but become synonymous with "organic."

Most whey sold is about muscle building and high protein content is all they are looking for. This is just not our objective. It seemed that you got this in your earlier post. But I just want to make this clear for the group. The HL MSM and Low Carb Diet key-in quite nicely to this and all can make a huge improvement to your life in ways that most have no idea about.

In fact, you may actually age backwards for a spell... imagine that! I did in many ways. If you read my book, I give you some references. My hair is lighter... not grey, but lighter. Certainly, I have higher energy levels than at age 56 and my skin has improved. My nails grow at alarming rates... seems like they need cutting every four days. And I just never am ill or even out of sorts. This is just a very different way to live than I previously imagined.

I was sitting with a guy my age last night who had arranged his funeral and grave plot. I can't imagine even thinking like this. With no health problems, why? He had three bypasses and was racked with arthritis. No! This is just not in my game plan. I am a much better man now than at age 56 when I discovered HL MSM. So do it right and reestablish your outlook as a young person per Dr. . That is what you will be even if you are 72 like me.

So I agree with Alobar's suggested question. The qualities occur after Undenatured Whey Isolate ingestion when a chain of interesting events take place that help do things like fix holes in your gut and completely overhaul nutrient paths. The CCO archives are loaded with these discussions also if you are interested.

By the way, Duncan Crow may be lost in the mountains somewhere, but he is still within range of emails. You can talk to him and he is still making a living in supplement sales and with advice. He is quite knowledgeable if you need it.

Kind Regards, HUuman

On 7/16/2014 12:45 AM, Alobar > Alobar
>
> On Tue, Jul 15, 2014 at 10:58 PM, sk [coconut_oil_open_forum] <coconut_oil_open_forum@yahoogroups.com > wrote:
>

glutathione

> I just typed in Glutathione beside the proteins that should produce Glutathione being cold-processed & undenatured. Not sure if I liked the concentrate, so I skipped that one. I think the best Whey is the Life Source as they make it in small batches with LOTS of great qualities.

I'm just trying to get some HQ protein at the best price possible. :)
> Take care, Keith

The cheapest and best source of this is Undenatured Whey Isolates.

Get the Genetic Test

Hi Joe:

Why do you not get a 23 & Me test ($99) and find out what is really causing this imbalance?

I love Standard Process stuff, but you are working in the blind till you could actually know the real story.

The MTHFR level may not get it though. A higher level test may be the ticket. The point is that you are working at an antiquated level with hair tests. They only tell you the chemistry and they are not very accurate, as several here have posted in the past.

The real cure may be high levels of say, methyl B12, but who knows? While your C therapy may have some effects, it is not getting the real job done. A raised copper level indicates a genetic defect, most likely, at some critical juncture. As you know, I am just learning this and have no idea what that might be, but we now have these tools and you are not applying them.

On 7/16/2014 7:28 AM, Joe [coconut_oil_open_forum] wrote:

> *I just had an HTMA (hair mineral analysis) done and was told again that I have copper imbalance / deficiency, and too much free copper. Morley told me the key to my healing this might be by taking 750-1000 mg of WFVC [whole food vitamin C], made by SP (Standard Process). I want to merge my HTMA program with magnet therapy, and I may choose to take these doses of WFVC vs megadosing on Sodium Ascorbate like I'm doing right now, because 750 to 1000 mg of WFVC might have more effect than 20 grams of Na Asc. It's all Standard Process stuff, and that's all made to rebalance*

people very efficiently. If you have a healer that uses SP and knows how to prescribe it, you have a very good thing. I've always wanted one, and I now have it.
>Joe

Adapting to the MSM Taste

This problem is probably the biggest one standing between total wellness and most of those who flounder. I have explained that swishing with water gets the job done and that when you do it the best thing to do is find a project like washing dishes and swish till the last dish is washed. By then, you will have forgotten all about the MSM and there is no real taste to contend with. What I don't recommend is mixing MSM with juices as many try.

First off, the juices will not taste at all good in the quantities that you'll finally need to be taking. Second, you simply absorb this stuff in your mouth... and the methyl groups kill the taste buds pretty well when you swish.

So what is swishing? After putting a tablespoon of MSM in your mouth, followed by water: It is a combination of chewing the crystals and moving it back and forth in your mouth. Hey, people have been doing this for hundreds of years with shot of liquor. It works there and it works here. If you think MSM tastes badly... try drinking a shot of bourbon straight down (maybe not, just a comparison). Bourbon is poison and this is the very best food in the world for western people, but the idea is the same. The taste kinda disappears when you swish. "Now deal the cards please..." Alobar

Hi Ege:

Sounds like a good plan... thanks Alobar.

Interestingly, no one told me about any of this. I just started taking massive amounts and it worked just fine after the horse farmer gave me the rundown and a bucket of MSM from his railcar. I had taken one gram amounts like everyone else and gotten, basically zero benefits along with Glucosamineand and Chondroitin (also sulfates, but not available in any large amounts without stomach distress)... which means that you are not maybe getting so much worse, but you are not improving either.

The farmer had me so juiced with his story that I would have injected it with a syringe just to get what he was suggesting. Well, the rest is history.

This new information that the others have brought into the group like Paul and Mike on methylation just tell us why all of this is so dynamite. Then you add Dr. Stephanie Seneff's videos on what she knows about organic sulfur... no, you can get sulfur from a few other sources, but it is nothing like it once was, historically. The lack of organic sulfur in our greens is why we are dying of first, joint disease, then heart problems, as we progressively deteriorate.

To me, we should be teaching our kids what Alobar is telling you... everyone should be taking at least small amounts of MSM, even as small children. Mothers pass on sulfur as part of their own prenatal nourishment, we eat some, and by the time we reach 45-50 it is all gone. Then, we all gather up our walkers and begin our long painful trek to the graveyard. That journey can take 30-40 years and it is much slower than it should be, nowadays. Oldsters today are far sicker than they have ever been and chock full of drugs in the process.

So even though you have a good part of the way out with HL MSM, please don't lose site of the Whey and Low Carb Diet complements. Whey is also a sulfur source. Learn them all, but always learn them slowly. All dietary changes and supplements cause stress and they should be done with caution. I am just grateful that I found Duncan and his whey program and that we all learned about the devastating effects of sugar (and carbs).

There is plenty more, but this is a good start.

Kind Regards, Huuman

On 7/16/2014 3:43 PM, Alobar [coconut_oil_open_forum] wrote:
> *Start small. Maybe 1/4 tsp. Taste is indeed wretched. But after a week or so, the body will grok the health benefits and the taste will slowly go from utterly wretched to not so bad. Drink plenty of water so you will have lots and lots of saliva*

to secrete around the MSM.
> As your taste buds adjust, increase your MSM dose. Currently I take about 2 Tblsp per dose.
> Alobar
>

Good to hear about your finger Tre... I figured it'd work, but you never know. I had a friend in the Air Force whose thumb swelled up and looked real bad. So guess what? The Air Force Doctors in their wisdom, just cut it off!!! Yup... amputated it and threw it in the trash.

He showed me the stump about a week afterwards... blew me away.

Thanks... And Another Healing

On 7/16/2014 3:18 PM, Tre [coconut_oil_open_forum] wrote:

> On 7/16/2014 3:18 PM, Tre [coconut_oil_open_forum] wrote:
>>
>> Hi I just started taking cell food, an oxygen and trace minerals supp, along with msm for joint enlargement for a dislocated finger joint. It is working to reduce the swollen joint and now there is no discomfort/pain there. My fingers were beginning to rotate also. I want to stop this joint deformity.

>> Lymeover

>>lymeover.com "Natural forces within us are the true healers of disease" - Hippocrates. So our own far-infra red is produced and sent into us with variable temperatures. Ask today how this can happen.

>>Thank you, Jim. When msm alone was not helping I wanted this to be in the history records here in this group.

>>Thank you for your time and experience and constant sharing.

>>Sad for your friend. I wish more people would be more open to learning of their deficiencies before resorting to such final things as throwing away and hurting parts of themselves. When we lose parts they are forever lost. We are not lizards that regrow tails. Maybe, someday, science will manipulate us to be able to clone all extremity and organ parts. Bionic is coming...

>>Lymeover

>> On Jul 16, 2014, at 9:06 AM, "'Cherwyn'[coconut_oil_open_forum]" <coconut_oil_open_forum@yahoogroups.com> wrote:

>>> *Are you all familiar with Dr. Kharrazian's glutathione supplements, Oxy-Cell and such? (By Apex.)*
>>> *What are your thoughts on these? I was taking them for*

a while as part of the AutoImmune Protocol to heal the gut.

>>> I think that anytime anyone suggests raising glutathione levels to a general population, a "caveat emptor" ought to be given to those with cancer who are using chemotherapy to combat the cancer. Elevated glutathione levels can cause resistance of cancer cells to chemotherapy.

http://onlinelibrary.wiley.com/doi/10.1002/cbf.1149/abstract;jsessionid=3DF88354C4219CDDD3BC158286AE3FB3.f04t01?deniedAccessCustomisedMessage=&userIsAuthenticated=false

>>>
http://informahealthcare.com/doi/abs/10.1080/10408360500523878

Niacin Vs. Niacinimide

(Niacin is another B vitamin that is often taken in large amounts and certainly it has its application, but this also generally goes against this new Unified Medicine)

On Thu, Jul 17, 2014 at 12:28 PM, hope [coconut_oil_open_forum] <coconut_oil_open_forum@yahoogroups.com> wrote:

I've used niacin and niacinimide. Any opinions on which is safer? Thanks in advance!

"Niacin: Too Dangerous for Routine Cholesterol Therapy"

Hi Hope

> On Thu, Jul 17, 2014 at 12:28 PM, hope-one [coconut_oil_open_forum] <coconut_oil_open_forum@yahoogroups.com> wrote:

> *I take a heaping TBLSP of Niacin daily. I am diabetic and the Niacin flush helps to reduce the size of my swollen legs. Good for preventing blood clots.*

> *My #1 trusted source of vitamin info is* **http://www.doctoryourself.com/index.html**. *They claim that there are no deaths from vitamins.*

Dr Andrew W. Saul, Alobar's trusted #1 man, known as "the megavitamin man" has been advocating megsdoses of vitamins for 38 years... Needless to say, he is not into METYLATION therapies yet. LOL

Hi All:

If you just study the methylation cycles you will see immediately that these two forms of B vitamins are not the same and that both have their uses.

Also, as I posted some time ago: Large doses of niacin may

have their application, but what Alobar is doing is certainly not for everyone. High dose niacin can exacerbate methylation cycle problems, especially those with MTHFR anomalies (and this includes a large segment of the people in the US and especially those of Spanish decent).

I am just waiting for the day that Alobar tells us that his Type II is gone and he has no more signs of it. Given his dedication to natural healing and his knowledge, I am expecting it. To date, no one has ever reported that HL MSM has assisted them in getting rid of this Type II affliction (despite the online claims with small amounts).

I am not sure if Type II should be called a disease, since it is not pathogenic... but all of medical terms probably should be reconsidered in light of some of the recent information. Also, as per my earlier post and the videography herein, nothing may actually be "caused" by pathogens. Really understanding this whole nutritive/pathogenic relationship could actually redefine the idea of what disease is. Drug companies are not helping in this as they sell their products based on ludicrous and biased information.

I would love to hear some discussion on this from the group. There are some very interesting posts on this topic in our CCO records if you research them. Also, the newsletter "Crusador" referenced above reported on this topic a few years back. This month's copy, by the way, has a great summary on Organic Sulfur and C for those interested.

http://www.247wereport.com/ I recommend their newsletter and also, some of their products are pretty unique and not so available elsewhere. Also, they generally sell organic supplements only which meet this new standard of science.

Mainstream Tests Niacin... B-Vitamins

On 7/18/2014 11:20 PM, Alobar (moderator) [coconut_oil_open_forum] wrote:
> I wrote to Doc Saul of the Orthomolecular Medicine Foundation. He did a video on FB debunking the news report.

>
https://www.facebook.com/photo.php?v=265980030275194

> Alobar
>>
> On Thu, Jul 17, 2014 at 1:58 PM, Alobar> wrote:
>
> I think the website is nuts! I suspect the deaths the cardiologist reported were from the prescription drugs he prescribed.
> I take a heaping TBLSP of Niacin daily. I am diabetic and the Niacin flush helps to reduce the size of my swollen legs. Good for preventing blood clots.
> My #1 trusted source of vitamin info is:
http://www.doctoryourself.com/index.html.

They claim that there are NO deaths from vitamins.
\>   *Alobar*

First off, the idea that there is such a thing as "cholesterol therapy" is incorrect as Tans has said here repeatedly and virtually everyone here agrees. What do you take for hemoglobin therapy? Same idea.

This entire discussion is driven by the trillion dollar "statin" market that is founded on false pretenses and must to be taken down. Please follow what we are saying here and you will do well, I promise, without drugs. I have gotten hundreds of letters attesting to this.
Very funny video, Alobar.

I don't recommend singlet vitamins per this book, but these reports are crazy. Certainly, this is a great example of mainstream ignorance. Andrew Saul's report is right on and everyone here should watch it. We know for a fact that the entire B-vitamin complement is key to the methylation sequence working properly in most people. That is certain: Genetically compromised people are actually negatively affected by the things that make the rest of the population healthy and we must be aware of this concern.

In any case, the key is to never make multiple nutritional changes at once, to pay careful attention to any that you make, and to get your nutritional needs from whole foods where possible (as Saul says, here).

To Hope's question: You are asking which of two B vitamins are better and the answer is that we need them both. As Alobar says, there are commonly no deaths from any vitamins and maybe three a year from supplements of all kinds. Now compare that to the many thousands a year that always occur from MD prescribed drugs.

Still, the bottom line here, I hope, is to be at the top of our games and not just survival. The tests are there to tell us how much. If you take any vitamins, use only organic (contain methyl groups). Most of what I take is herbal... things like moringa, Maca, etc. or simply foods like HL MSM and Undernatured Whey Isolates.

If you are doing everything correctly, your circulatory system will be pliable and your blood will be correct for your biology, Blood tests will be a waste of time and expense for you. In fact medical testing in general is ill advised unless you have good reason and you know how the test works. Few insitu tests are benign.

Finally, if you have done the genetic tests and it is determined that you are expressing certain genetic defects, then you may actually need to take large doses of certain organic B-vitamins. However, without them, you are a blind man without a cane. Do your homework and know what you are doing. I notice that Saul never discusses this.

> > I've used niacin and Niacinimide. Any opinions on which is safer?

> From what little I know, they are both 'safe,' but do different things... Niacin will cause dilation of the tiny capillaries that are mainly close to the surface of your skin. This is what causes the 'niacin flush' that people who take larger doses of niacin experience (I find it almost pleasurable, others find it uncomfortable).

> Niacinimide, on the other hand, supposedly causes dilation of the larger blood vessels, which causes a weird, creepy-crawly feeling deep inside your body - which is supposed to be very good for the internal organs.

> I don't think there is any hard science to back this up, and I can't recall where I learned this, but it was a long time ago when I was researching this subject, so take it with a grain of salt.

> Tanstaafl

Differences between the B's

Hi Tans:

I would say that you are correct down to the "no Hard Science part." We are not there yet, of course, but we are worlds closer than we were 15 years ago. In another 15, I am guessing, those paying attention will have it all nailed.

I would have agreed with you completely last year, though.

Methylation vs What Works

On 7/18/2014 10:31 PM, Alobar [coconut_oil_open_forum] wrote:
> *I would say "like a medicine" not "like a drug." Perhaps I am being semantically picky. Big Pharma pushes drugs. Tobacco is a drug. Etc.*
> *Alobar*

Hi Alobar:

Yes, you are, Alobar, if I may be so bold. This is now pure science, not just semantics. Moreover, this is a key point in these new methylation therapies that Paul has led us into. Watch the videos and get on board. You need not be tested to understand them and know that they must work as advertised.

Virtually every doctor with this new expertise will state what I am saying. The reason is that now, for the first time in history, we can actually test and "know" which vitamin (etc.) and how much. The entire idea makes what you are suggesting (high dose anything), hocus pocus. We are no longer guessing my friend. When you squeeze the trigger, the gun fires in the direction pointed. The charts tell you what happens when and how.

That said, genetic expression and history are keys to this new science. Also, if what you are doing is already working, I would certainly take my time to make any changes, if any. This is about self-awareness and paying attention.

The bottom line in all of this is Epigenetics. Therefore, even if the actual supplements that you are taking do nothing for most people, if you can them make work for you and you are happy with them, party on! These same above doctors agree that you must not upset the applecart. The idea here is that changes incur stress and stress causes inflammation, which creates disease. You simply avoid throwing out the baby with the wash. Our goal is wellness, not following any protocol.

In fact, if you'll notice, I now agree that there are no such things as protocols. When you think about it, there just cannot be a single way of doing anything that fits all biological entities (us). The whole idea of a single protocol makes absolutely no sense. Still I will continue to call the HL MSM, Undenatured Whey, and Low carb Diets Protocols, as they work for most of us. Nothing in the applications has changed, but certainly the emphasis has.

If you will notice also, while I may have given the above lip service in "It's the Liver Stupid," I am much more firm in my grasp of what is going on today and why as study this. I also understand why they are saying these things. Before, it was more of a hunch and now we have the proof right here in our hands.

The Ultimate Quantum Machine

Our bodies are basically machines of nature... a 30% efficient machine is and will always be very, very good at this material level of science. That is, under what we have accepted as Newtonian laws. But don't kid yourself... there is more and we are all over this solution today.

There are quantum methods of raising these outcomes and they will come. I have proven it myself. My own cars have shown 150mpg and double the power. These same simple methods will affect our bodies, and in the same way, as I have said previously here. HL MSM is a quantum step in that direction, but there is plenty more work to do. My first book gave you the mechanics and this one the science, which is now all over the web in one form or another. Eventually, when truth is known, it just creeps out, despite what big pharma and its pseudoscience does to stop it.

Some here may have heard of the people... "the God Eaters"... who take in no food and simply absorb the quantum energy of space. Do they exist? I have already seen enough to know that they could and accept the notion. The first step in making anything happen physically is to believe that it can and b open to it.

This is how the new science, Epigenetics, actually works. It is the science of spirituality in effect. The idea that through visualization and dreams, we can change outcomes. And now science has come to realize, to its disgruntlement, that we actually do this, finally. The more that we get this out, the closer we will get to an ideal solution.

This is a progression that takes time. Certainly, if we make ourselves disease-free as a population, it would put a huge strain on what we now use in materials and energy. This would be the ultimate solution to this progression... death only by accident (and maybe by retrieval, as we do away with that, as I think Osh suggested earlier) and no food consumption. As Dan Nelson will tell you, a cubic inch of space can power everything on earth through quantum devices.

I am not sure what would kill us in this scenario, but I am quite confident that we will not live forever on this earth, no matter what. This is just too harsh an environment for highly refined Souls as we move up the spiritual ladder. So, as I see it, we will die of our own accord and devices. That is how it should happen in my opinion. When we have reached a certain level of spiritual unfoldment, we just say goodbye to our friends and family, close our eyes and move on. This all makes death into a very lovely experience and nothing negative.

This should not be a planet of wars, unreasonable pain, or tremendous struggles for those who have learned how to avoid them. It should be one of love and the understanding that this unqualified love is our goal. Still, there will always be those who doubt everything and struggle through life with pain and misfortune. Those are the new Souls who must learn the ropes and this is a great place to learn them.

So Osh... I think that you can see that my idea of nature is that it is quite imperfect, but we as Quantum Beings are not. I hope that you can buy into this with me. Somehow, I think that you can.

Kind Regards, HUuman

On 7/17/2014 1:46 PM, olushola[coconut_oil_open_forum] wrote:

- > I can't believe this! Nature is not so imperfect. Now it may be true in our modern society where our gut has been compromised by the agribusiness, big pharma, drinking water, etc.
>
> Olushola
>
> On Thu, Jul 17, 2014 at 11:38 AM, Jim[coconut_oil_open_forum] <coconut_oil_open_forum@yahoogroups.com> wrote:
>
Good point Osh... but really: The best gut in the world is probably no better than about 30% efficient and that is better

than the best internal combustion engines when you get to the bottom line.

> Posted by: olushola

The best Whey... Again/ Lemons

Hi Tans:

> You have argued in the past that it is better to get your 'vitamin C'
from foods like lemons. Lemons are a food, so that is a perfectly valid statement, and one that I agree with.

I consider an organic lemon to be an absolute superfood when the peel is consumed along with it. They would rate a 10 on a 10 scale in my book, only HL MSM rates higher, Unlike MSM, lemons are for "everyone" and MSM does not work for those with the CBS +/+ defect (maybe 1/100 people).

Incidentally, to your comment specifically referring to 'undenatured whey isolates'...

What I do know is that I have been using Now Brand Whey in very high quantities for several years (2-3 times what Duncan recommends) and I am more healthy than any 72 yr old, probably, on this planet. I play a wicked game of tennis and never am winded, my sex drive is thru the roof... higher than at age 30, and life is a ball.

The point here is: Something is working my friend... maybe the whey does not even count, but I like it. Maybe it is all about the HL MSM and related supplements. Do I really care? Should I be looking this gift horse in the mouth as you are? One thing for sure is that the Whey is not poisoning me.

Now I am totally pain free and happy as a tick on a big dog. Just tell me where I am going wrong please. I have never been ill or even tired in over five years... no colds, nothing. I don't even get sunburn anymore when I am overexposed to the sun. It was never this good, even as a kid. Even then, I had juvenile arthritis, was getting cavities in my teeth, my fingers would get stiff in a snowball fight, and I would sunburn on occasion.

> So, unless/until you or Duncan or someone else can rebut - with evidence - my claim that whey protein that comes from pasteurized milk (like your NOW brand) IS DENATURED, at least to an extent, stands.

Duncan went to his NZ brand for valid reasons. He got me onto Now Whey and I love the taste. I am not inclined to believe that your brand has anything about it to that make me drop their product, but I have not even tried it because it costs more and I am happy with Now.

However, don't get me wrong, I may try yours and switch in a heartbeat. I am never stuck. Change is a part of my religion, really. I am always willing to change... nothing owns me. I have found that if I keep an open mind, spirit always seems to guide me in the right direction. I love that.

The Quantum Beings Known as People

On 7/20/2014 11:49 AM, olushola camara camaramahawa@gmail.com [coconut_oil_open_forum] wrote:

So Osh... I think that you can see that my idea of nature is that it is quite imperfect, but we as Quantum Beings are not...

Hmm, this seems contradictory, since we are derived from nature. Of course it depends on how one defines nature.

I hope that you can buy into this with me. Somehow, I think that you can...

>I keep an open mind and always challenge my paradigms as that is the only way to climb that ladder to being a Quantum Human; the ancients of Nile valley civilization called it Sons of Light.
Olushola"

Hi Osh:

We are now on my very favorite topic, Osh, as you might guess by my first book, and I love your attitude as usual. I believe that this ties in closely to Epigenetics and wellness in ways that few have yet begun to grasp. I just hope that a better mainstream grasp of all of this is coming soon as we get the word out here.

Yes, Osh, it does depend on the definition. Good point.

When you begin a spiritual conversation (and in many ways this all becomes the same thing), as I am sure you are aware, terminology becomes very important. Also, how many different protestant churches in Christianity are there? Why?

To me, religions are jamming observations and ideas that want to be (are trying to be real), but are seemingly unbelievable events, placed into a format that our little minds can grasp. Quantum events are a great example of what religion is attempting to discuss, but really can't get across, so they come across as invalid to many as they are told.

Epigenetics tell us that we can heal ourselves, not only physically, but mentally, with our attitudes. Does this sound like a religious topic? So now we can say with confidence and from a proven scientific viewpoint that love can heal you and it is not a leap, really, once you get what is going on. So isn't this really what they were trying to say all along? Now we know it is all real stuff and it works... no parables needed!

Now, dropping back: Which came first, nature or us (as Soul)? Did we create all of this or did It create us? I tend to believe the first. I doubt many here agree, so far, but that is my contention. Proving this would make us far more powerful than religions give us credit for. My impression is that we are all little Gods under a larger envelop and maybe many larger ones. That would make It like a galaxy in Universe. Maybe they go on forever? That would be cool.

A step further... we are not just us, the people of earth and here is why:

Realize that anything at the Quantum level can occur in two places at once and this has been proven time and again by experiment. Quantum Electrodynamics today is the most reliable science that we have as Dan Nelson will tell you. The reason is that it is always repeatable and there are no real conflicts once you grasp what is happening.

Conversely, Newtonian Science is "shot fulla holes my friend." Try gravity as a beginning and work from there. Electricity? Are you kidding? Conflicts are everywhere. So when you get small, things get real... but not more obvious.

Quantum Physics results are counter-intuitive and really, unbelievable. This, because we are just not observing particles at this level enough to grasp or predict what they will do next. It all becomes almost dream-like.

Why only two levels at once? Because no one has devised an experiment to prove more. I suggest that we are multilevel beings that appear here on earth as a single body... a quantum concept.

Dreaming is a simple example. We commonly only realize our physical body because that is our present focus and that is what most of us only see. So what happens when you die? I contend that you let go of one body. Death, then, and even life, would be an illusion that we all agree to and accept as our reality.

So here, this claim that we are Quantum Beings becomes huge once you grasp the implications.

Kind Regards, HUuman

Why Take Breaks?

On 7/20/2014 11:10 AM, Tanstaafl tanstaafl@libertytrek.org [coconut_oil_open_forum] wrote:
>
> On 7/19/2014 2:23 PM, Jim Clark jrcarchitectde@gmail.com wrote: (Snipped)

I am knocking any high dose vitamin taken blindly, period. (I explain why in the water discussion herein in detail)

>*Tans: You are the largest proponent of HL MSM out there, are you not?*

There are very few, if any, who understand this fully, so yes. However, there are a two on You Tube who get a part of it.

>Tans: In context, MSM is a 'vitamin', just like Niacin, or Ascorbic acid.

In the context of? I never take breaks on HL MSM and have taken it for over fifteen years. Sometimes I take 3 tblpns/ day if I have strained something playing tennis... others just one.

I never take a break on Whey either. Why would you?

>Tans: Because with most things, if you don't, your body gets too used to it, and starts leaning more and more heavily on the external source as time goes on.

Everyone on the farm ate eggs every day for their entire lives. Did they get used to them? I agree, generally, with your recommendation and basis. I just find that these two are way too close to perfect foods to fit this. I say, never stop feeding your methylation cycles at their critical junctures unless you have a genetic defect that tells you to do otherwise.

While I did not invent the MSM protocol, as far as I know, my book and I were the "only" spokesman for it, and still are, for the most part, except for the many members of CCO who have seen benefits from it. When you read about MSM elsewhere, they are always discussing maximum one (or so) gram amounts. My finding is that taking it in high levels increases its outcome at least a hundred fold and even a tspn/day will hardly be noticed.

Historically, I have also lived on a limited range of foods other than fruit and berries, which I eat as they seasonally appear. When I get onto a pattern of eating that suites, I follow it. But we are all creatures of habit. The clue here is to make any habits beneficial ones.

The wife is a gourmet cook and always is dropping new foods on me and sometimes to my displeasure, since she tends to follow recipes. Most people (and the FDA) have no clue what is healthful, she will use harmful oils, etc in her dishes just as those who wrote the recipes. I actually throw away corn oil every so often, but she gets a recipe and buys more. At least now, she has stopped frying foods, but she still sautes them. Cooking is a huge creative outlet for her and we all need outlets, so I allow cheating.

When you look at the methylation charts, it is clear that anything that helps supply glucosamine is critical and that is the point with whey. The same goes for organic sulfur and the methyl groups that MSM supplies. Other than for the few CBS impaired, these hit the nail squarely on the head. You simply cannot do any better, I was absolutely lucky to have picked those two nutrients out of the basket. I do accept divine guidance as a real possibility here.

I say that you will not likely ever find a better fit for most people than these two basic protocols. The same goes for the Low carb diet, but that is becoming commonly known and understood for its obvious benefits.

Quantum... It's Really All About:

On 7/22/2014 8:31 PM, olushola [coconut_oil_open_forum] wrote:
>
> There are machines that measure what our device does on cars, so quantum reactions are clearly measurable using Newtonian level devices such as gas gauges. Not sure if that refutes your point or agrees, but if I put a quantum device on my car and it shows an increase in performance. Is that what you mean?
>
> Okay, I see you are talking about QED. My exposure to quantum physics came through the brief study of astrophysics, which is quite different from QED. Anyway, **http://physics.about.com/od/quantumphysics/p/quantumphysics.htm** gives a good overview of the fields of quantum phenomenon.

Hi Osh and All:

Dan Nelson, who I learned about from a member of this CCO Group a couple of years ago, Mary Jane Helms, is an AstroPhysicist. Please take some time and listen to him if you have not. He is a mind blower for sure. I have quoted him here often and recommend his reverse laser water that she told us about then.

When I discovered Dan, my friend Rich and I were right in the middle of this QED CoilPack4U experimentation. Rich is now very well versed in what Dan teaches when it comes to quantum healing. Rich is an amazing person and healer in his own right and is now way too busy with this work to even talk to me much, anymore. He has helped several people here in the CCO group since. I recommended him (no guarantees and I make nothing from his work).

Yes, QED is probably the most reliable science that we have per Dan and I have to say that it has spun my brain around a few times with our findings on cars. If you have not looked at it, watch our videos on **http://coilpack4u.com/**. There is no denying that the results that we have seen are game changers and once believed and understood will be worth a fortune. But my interest at the moment is in my architectural work which has really picked up, plus, getting this latest book out.

I would say that any exposure to QED and Quantum Physics puts you right up there at the head of the pack. You just can't know about this stuff and be closed-minded. My vision is to open the mind, then open the heart. When that happens, healing begins to occur at all levels and we can all use some of that.

These are far greater than anything I can offer. That is, what I am normally discussing here such as these protocols or what I consider a Quantum Leap... Methylation. When you are in pain, your consciousness tends to focus just on just that. So, first, alleviate the pain, then you can put your full attention on spirituality. Then I have reached my goal... to allow everyone here the option to grasp the real reason that you, as Soul, even exist.

Agreements/ Closing Group Thoughts

On 7/21/2014 11:09 AM, Joyce[coconut_oil_open_forum] wrote:
>
> Jim, I just want to say that at times some of the people on the forum get really testy, take things personally and above all lose sight of all the hard work, effort and humor you put into this great and informative forum. We are all humans yes, but also very individual and unique in how we manifest and express health, wellness, happiness and diseases/illnesses.

>People should stop and listen first before going on and on about how so is wrong and he or she is right... In the short time I've spent on the forum, I've learned plenty (4 weeks) so much so that **I healed my left shoulder** that left me not able to do many exercises I enjoyed such as Pullups and certain yoga poses. Thanks to the MSM and whey protocol within less than two weeks I'm one happy climber & poser:) To boot, my hormone issues was greatly alleviated and I **lost about 7 pounds** in the whole process. I'm one of several benefactors

of Jim's protocol without spending one cent on a doctor. To me that is the beauty of discovering great finds such as this forum. Live and learn :)

> We don't have to all agree on the same things but listening, experimenting, trying and paying attention instead of getting all dogmatic about this can be a bonus to all concern. I can see the hard work some of the people who have been on the forum for a long time. We all want the same things, so if such and such vitamins, latest gadget or find works for you fabulous! Share it so some people can try it and see what happens.
> I look forward to trying more of your recommendations and will keep you posted on how their working but so far so great not just good!
> Joyce

> Again, Jim, thank you for all your efforts. I know someday soon you will be validated

> On Jul 21, 2014, at 4:56 PM, Jim huuman42@gmail.com [coconut_oil_open_forum] wrote

Hi Joyce and All:

Thank you Joyce for your kind words... you are just a lovely woman with a great attitude. You lighten up the room with your presence and I am so happy that you have seen these benefits. I will be looking for your face at the 2086 reunion

Joyce, keep up the good work my friend.

Interesting Agreement in the Breast Study

I am at this minute reading the June/ July issue of Crusador, a bimonthly newsletter that I have recommended in the past. The current Front page issue is "Sulfur & Vitamin C" and how they work together to increase the benefits of MSM (as they call it, organic sulfur). It is not yet posted on their site, but they include some new words that parrot what I have been saying here and in my book. This is the first time that I have come across the implications here. They imply that HL MSM is more effective against breast cancer than lower levels as follows and I quote:

"In this study, we demonstrated that **MSM substantially decreased** the viability of **human breast cancer cells** in a **"dose dependent"** manner (More is better, then... they are getting it!)

So what I was taught by the horse farmer is catching on and this is a quote from the mainstream study. As it was done on mice, not people, doses are impossible to translate into human terms.

Finally, this entire article basically states exactly what I have been telling the people here for about seven or eight years with regard to **arthritis and joint ailment**, but also with regard to inflammation, PMS, hair growth, skin disorders, allergies, and cancer prevention. However, in all of these cases, the dose was so low that it would hardly matter compared to what I have found to be true. That is, three grams/ twice a day is just not a therapeutic level (even if it is three times normal amounts). Never do they discuss the possibility of it curing autoimmune disease or some of the things reported here by others.

Now these people sell MSM for many times what it costs them and theirs is probably not as good as the AniMed that I recommend. In fact, as a recent horse farmer just agreed a month or so ago, the stuff AniMed sells is indeed the highest quality MSM available. I explain why in our CCO Achieves and also in my book, "It's the Liver Stupid."

For them to recommend two heaping tablespoons/day would probably sound like they were out to make a killing (and they would at this rate). I have nothing to gain from what I have discovered. I just know that for arthritis, two heaping tablespoon/ day is really a minimum therapeutic amount for people over about 45 years old. But we are all dose dependent individuals. However, as I have always said, start low and work up gradually. This is good advice for any therapeutic food and it includes the whey protein protocol.

So if you have extra time on your hands to read, look up the Crusador site and read their various newsletters. These are very good health reports and they are free.

Kind Regards, HUuman

Memory (???)

Hi Craig:

Thanks for affirming this. Memory is such an interesting thing.

I can recall in third grade spending hours studying a list of ten really easy spelling words and never really getting them down. My Mom would go over them time and again. I kept spelling tired tird and she would laugh.

Now I meet a new person, ask them their name and forget it almost as soon as they say it, but I come here and recall a name from ten years ago.

Duncan went over his stuff sometimes only once and it was stuck in my mind and still is after eight years. What is with that? Will we ever have a combination of nutrients or a genetic fix to patch this weirdness? I would be grateful if we did, but I am also grateful for being able to go back more than seventy years to scenes on my Grandmother's front porch with my kiddy cart (a sort of wooden tricycle without pedals that I loved then). How does this tie-into "The Science of Belief Video" p34 and what Rob Williams teaches?

I attribute the memory holes to heavy metal poisoning, but I'll never know for certain. I do know that I had my first amalgam filling at age five and that included nitrous oxide. I can recall sitting through that experience in the dental chair like it was yesterday. Now, today, I think back and ask why would anyone fill a baby tooth with poison? Did the ADA actually want to keep us stupid?

So we now know that both nitrous oxide and mercury are both poisons. That dentist gave me some of his mercury poison to take home and play with (I think just to make sure that I got an adequate dose). Today, if the EPA knew that you had loose mercury in your house like that, they would declare it a hazard zone and send a crew in white suites to clean it up.

Things have changed, but in most ways, they have gotten far worse than they were then.

Cheers, HUuman

On 7/23/2014 1:30 PM, crgstef@aol.com [coconut_oil_open_forum] wrote:
>
> Jim - You are entirely correct. I'm just surprised that someone with such a keen mind didn't recall Duncan's recommendations on Cataracts.

> Regards,
> Craig

Keen mind? Well thanks Craig. Think about it. You recall the info on what affects you. Chances are extremely good that I will never have cataracts... but this ties into the above memory post.

Hi Tans:

If you would please look at these: PubMed, Dr. Murry, NYU... (the first three searches that Google gave me by the way). There are plenty of good outcomes even though these all used far too small of amounts to show anything like what we are seeing with my protocol in our CCO group. However, they are not inconsequential.

Furthermore, I submit that MSM (in small amounts) is far, far better known than the Whey Protein Isolate Protocol that Duncan Crow gave us when he was active here. His site is very specific as to how the Whey Protocol works and what the outcomes are. This is not at all about using whey as a protein enhancement. It is about glutathione and how it helps in the methylation cycle (again for most). This is not at all about little Miss Muffet, but indeed she is well known.

Also, while it takes some creativity to get there, I believe that you will easily see the obvious link between the methylation cycles and what two MSM or DMSO methyl groups will do for moving that needle (disregarding the few over-methylated). As to organic sulfur, it appears in many places in the cycles also, but please listen to Dr. Stephanie

Seneff's talks. Also, you may be busy and have little time for this, but you might even read my book before you further criticize what I have been telling others since 1998.

I noted that you had no comments regarding the recent MSM/breast cancer study on mice that got the group's attention. Why did you avoid the topic? Just interested, because that part has been very interesting to me and not inconsequential.

Since HL MSM got rid of several kinds of osteoarthritis arthritis for me including juvenile hip and finger varieties, I am sure that it works fine, despite your criticism below. However, no one ever made any claims that it cures crippling (rheumatoid) arthritis, although it appears to help to some degree. I would appreciate your telling me where you got this suggestion, please.

Finally, my own experience is that critics like yourself tend to be our best spokesmen when they get their heads on straight. Therefore, I welcome your efforts and commentary as long as you are actually doing the work that you claim. So far, you seem to have (as the song goes) searched in all the wrong places.

Kind Regards, HUuman

Please Read and Resubmit Your Report

>On 7/22/14 Tans :wrote:

> *Not sure what 'files' you are talking about re: evidence in support of HL MSM and Whey Protein having such a huge impact on health, but the evidence is all anecdotal - but substantial, and mounting every day.>*

> *Also, there is substantial mainstream evidence in support of the (whey protein isolate protocol, so you can't really lump the two together either.*
>
> *The fact is, if HL MSM can turn someone with crippling arthritis into someone having the joints of a 30-year old free from pain or discomfort, what would you call that?*

Hi Tans:

First, If you were willing to send me, say fifty million dollars, we could easily bring your concerns to a head (as the drug companies so readily do with far less valid products). Until then, we'll just have to go on with what those in the CCO Group reports and what the lower (what I consider non-therapeutic levels of MSM) do for people that are easily visited with Google on the web.

While these lower levels are not totally inconsequential, these doses did little for me prior to my being told about the HL MSM Protocol (as I named it in my first book), by the farmer in 1998. Since no labs are about to test HL MSM on mice or humans anytime soon (on purpose at any rate) these will just have to work for us till I/we can stir up interest elsewhere.

I'd really appreciate your help on this as I am sure that we are correct in our reports after five or more years of fairly comprehensive discussion in our group on these protocols and obviously spot on archives.

Please keep in mind that, so far, I believe that I may have had three people who could not actually do the HL MSM protocol at all. This being true, even though we know that (+/+) CBS cannot take organic sulfur or use additional methylation if their genetic defect is expressed.

We did have a healthcare pro in the CCO group about four years ago who could not use either protocol without problems. At the time, I was unaware of this CBS defect as was the rest of the world. I figured then that she was just being a crank. Now we know.

Taste is another matter. However, if you are hurting badly enough, you always will seem to manage to overcome that one. For some, like myself, this was never a factor. I was too interested in just getting well.

>>On 7/22/2014 12:50 AM, Tans wrote:

>> *Interestingly, I didn't trash the protocols either. I just stated they are not the hugely significant factors in healing disease as Jim states they are.*<<

Hi Tans:

I guess we can't really say what "hugely significant" means, so we'll leave this just as you state it, but cancer, PSC, fibro, arterial disease, and osteoarthritis are a start and these are actual volunteered and unsolicited by member's reports from our CCO group. (Yes, I have added several in this book, Mesothelioma... p43 should open some eyes).

Stick around and hear how others have benefitted in ways that go far beyond those available anywhere else. When the evidence is all in, my claims may be understated.

Or, if you have health issues, simple try these and you'll be reporting the benefits yourself. Especially, if you are over age 59 and have osteoarthritis or the joint deterioration that normally occurs in our population due to the low levels of organic sulfur commonly available.

Since joint heath improvement has become so commonplace with these, I am now more interested in hearing about the things that I never expected like cancer, fibro, and autoimmune cures, but it all helps prove them out and all will help advance this group and help us gain recognition.

These protocols work so well that they make challenges like these easy. We can only win from them.

Cheers, HUuman

On Cognitive Repair

Mike asks what to do for Cognitive Repair:

On 7/24/2014 8:36 AM, hope-one@live.com [coconut_oil_open_forum] wrote:
>
> Hi Mike:
>
> For cognitive repair, you need to supply the brain with raw materials it needs to repair the nervous system and enhance it. Take the lowest recommended dose of each and work your way up.

> Acetylcholine is crucial. To get the ACETYL portion, you can take acetyl-l-carnitine:

http://www.amazon.com/Carlson-Labs-Acetyl-L-Carnitine-Powder/DP/B003BVIV3I
> Take this supplement with the oils mentioned below. It will help your body absorb them better.

> For the CHOLINE, you can take choline citrate:
http://www.amazon.com/Serious-Nutrition-Solution-Choline-Citrate/DP/B007R87WPE/ref=sr_1_3?s=hpc&ie=UTF8&qid=1406204275&sr=1-3&keywords=choline+powder
> You also need Vitamin E, D and K. I would also take fish oil and cod liver oil. Here are the brands that I recommend. There may be better brands, but these are my

recommendations. Purchase as your budget allows:

> Vitamin E:
>http://www.amazon.com/Country-Life-Vitamin-Complex-2-Ounce/dp/B0013G8FCA/ref=sr_1_fkmr0_2?s=hpc&ie=UTF8&qid=1406205247&sr=1-2-fkmr0&keywords=natural+life+vitamin+e+moisturizing+creme

> D & K2:
http://www.amazon.com/THORNE-RESEARCH-Vitamin-Liquid-Health/dp/B0038NF8MG/ref=sr_1_5?s=hpc&ie=UTF8&qid=1406205156&sr=1-5

> Fish Oil:
http://www.amazon.com/Carlson-Finest-Liquid-Omega-3-Lemon/dp/B001LF39RO/ref=sr_1_1?ie=UTF8&qid=1406204761&sr=8-1&keywords=carlsons+fish+oil+lemon

> Cod Liver Oil:
http://www.amazon.com/Sonnes-Old-Fashioned-Cod-Liver/dp/B0011DL98M/ref=sr_1_1?ie=UTF8&qid=1406204792&sr=8-1&keywords=sonnes+cod+liver+oil

> I hope this helps,

> Hope

Hi Mike:

Cognitive repair comes with overall health... it is really all one thing and it all comes together on one package. But Hope has done a good job here.

Let me add especially first as top fats: Stop doing what the mainstream tells you, generally, when it comes to fats. No transfats, ever and animal fats are good for most all of us.

These are more general, some can't follow them:

- Stay away from deep fried foods, period,
- Eat nothing from packages (with a few exceptions, sardines are one).
- Start drinking whole milk and eating unprocessed dairy products...
- Free range eggs are great.
- Meat is fine, but don't trim off the fat and free range is the goal.
- Take Selenium
- Get plenty of C from organic lemon and grapefruit with skins
- Get the full complement of organic B vitamins and minerals
- Take no artificial vitamins or base minerals.
- Eat well, but never stuff yourself.
- Fresh berries are great.
- No artificial sugar, salt.
- Eat butter, not margarine or butter supplements.

Finally, most of our problems started in the fifties with Ancel Keys when he decided that cholesterol causes heart disease based on feeding it to rabbits!!! Also, get onto our whey, HL MSM protocols and the Low Carb Diet.

Regards, HUuman

MSM Video Lectures on You Tube

On 7/24/2014 4:15 PM, 'Janet [coconut_oil_open_forum] wrote (snipped):

> With regard to cataracts, Bill Rich explains here the mechanics of how MSM can prevent cataract formation: http://www.youtube.com/watch?v=kKdI3Dagfnk

> This is part 4 of a fascinating 7-part presentation (just over an hour in total) on the benefits of MSM for a wide range of ailments. I love this guy. I've watched the whole presentation 3 times now and I learn something new each time.

Janet

Hi Janet:

Yes, Bill has plenty to teach us with regard to MSM affects, but in terms of amounts, he is plain wrong, as are most on You Tube. I did find one pretty good one, below, but Bill is typical across the web today. They love the stuff, but have no idea how good it is and they will never know unless they step up their quantities.

Paraphrasing my first book: "So the finding is that eating peas cures cancer... and what do you do in response? You go on a three pea per day diet... woo, woo!"

Please note that Bill Rich is always discussing taking just 3 grams max. And unless you are around 25 years old and not really deficient (have a good store of organic sulfur), what he is discussing is just not going to be enough to do much of anything. My son needs a tablespoon at age 28 as do most his age today. He did OK at age 26 on 3 grams, though. Just listen to what your body says. He did, and now knows that his back will hurt if he is not at a tablespoon per day level. Always listen to what the body is saying and try to stay a few steps ahead.

Bill is way off the mark in dosage, but really good on discussing effects. So just listen to him and then multiply his results by twenty or thirty. And this is basically true for everyone, no matter how old you are. So Janet, if you find what Bill says to be fascinating, think about what your results will be by comparison. Yes, we are on another planet. Still, his results are very cool compared to drugs as everyone would agree.

Bill does have plenty of details to tell us that others miss and his dialogue is great. I am just glad that I ran into the MSM salesman/ horse farmer that I did instead of the veterinarian that he did (or I'd probably be dead now). As you can see in his video, he is probably aging normally, while slightly overweight. No, I am not being picky, but knowing what he does has not helped him stay young and it cannot do that in these amounts.

To his credit, he notes that we need other nutrients. While HL MSM is not "just a food," at three grams of MSM a day, it absolutely is just as he says.

Finally, Bill's topical application of MSM would do far better if he used DMSO, except that I would not use DMSO on poisons or bee stings.

There are many other videos on You Tube while you are here on this MSM topic that you should check out in addition. I mention a few below for various reasons:

Lion Heart Herbs is good and he has a very good handle on what we are discussing, so please, at a minimum, tune him in: **https://www.youtube.com/watch?v=PLtW_QM6mBk** He also "gets" how MSM helps methylation. Finally, he is well beyond the others here in terms of MSM ingestion and immediate effects.

Two other lecturers here are getting close to Lion Heart: Seth Williams who uses 10 grams, 2 teaspoons/ day and Neal's Yard **https://www.youtube.com/watch?v=hYSqyA4Y3nc** at

15 grams is getting there. Neal even mentions three heaping tablespoons at one point, but never really tells us why he goes there or why you should not also.

I call 15 grams a start, but nowhere near enough to make the therapeutic grade and grams are just not the correct way to measure MSM amounts. I really like using parts of a cup/day. Now you are thinking correctly. Measuring MSM in grams is like running a 240,000 inch race. Get your brain working at the correct scale, please.

So far, no one here in You Tube discusses swooshing which is a critical issue. Swishing gets the methylation process started right in your mouth. This means maximum absorption rates. Still, just a few years ago, there were no videos on this and none on higher levels, so it is progress.

Each lecturer here is very excited about his/her discovery with MSM. yet, they are bound to be comparatively benign at low rates. So listen to all these videos, multiply the effects where necessary, and get really excited about what I have been telling you. Be prepared to anti-age maybe ten years or more if you are fifty. In my case, it is difficult to evaluate because I was beating childhood problems in addition to the benefits of turning back years.

What I am now and have always advocated (well before You Tube even existed) is: if you are hurting (anywhere), swish much MSM as you can, and a ½ cup/ day level is certainly well within reason. Now that I am totally up to speed, I generally do two heaping tablespoons/ day, but sometimes only one, but I just never hurt anywhere. So there are no reminders.

By the way, the videos:
https://www.youtube.com/watch?v=rLsXgm28neA and **https://www.youtube.com/watch?v=MobDcOHWWb0** are simply incorrect on several points. One is that I take HL MSM on an empty stomach often and no problem. Also, taking it with juice is simply poor advice and it is a common work around that impairs MSM's ability to work in Methylation.

While everyone here takes and recommends MSM in varying amounts and they may take it in ways that limit the uptake and function, even bad advice will work to some degree with MSM. That is, it is very difficult to mess up when taking it. All you that you can really do in making mistakes is limit the good effects except with regard to releasing toxins (per the Lion Heart's video).

Finally, when you combine the three protocols in my book, they work together in ways that each cannot do separately, and, yes, organic C helps MSM work, just as moringa leaf helps soup-up whey.

Kind Regards, HUuman

Putting it Together / Using it Correctly

On 7/26/2014 10:37 AM, Joyce M [coconut_oil_open_forum] wrote

I want to add that maybe for some, when you start the HL MSM protocol with regard to hair, you will go through a detox effect meaning old weaker hair fall out and the regrowth are of a different texture (thicker, stronger and more lustrous).

I've always had good skin, but now it's even better. I can tell a big difference since using HL MSM that it has a better texture, softer, fine lines, and dark spots are disappearing. I was first worried that the hair shedding was the complete opposite of what MSM was suppose to do but my hairdresser said that the new growth are thicker strands and loads of baby hair! These are the effects I'm getting might be different for some people but MSM will most likely have an affect on hormonal issues due to better liver functioning etc.

I've used MSM before but never to such a high dosage and what even a tablespoon a day makes! If I've exercised heavily I take 2 tblspns the next day and no DOMS at all. I'm extremely grateful for discovering this along with the delicious whey smoothies.

I just received my Wayback Water all I can say is WOW! It really is incredible. It might seem like a lot of money but a

whole bottle can be used for three months but better to dose up as you start so you can get megahydrated then you can taper. The Wayback Water can be used for many things. I use on skin as a spray with drops of pure with essential oils and will try with diluted MSM.

Will get some DMSO and magnesium from seawater soon and will try them. I am sure that it is way cheaper and works better than some over-hyped and over-priced anti-aging creams in the market. I'm going to test it on bug bites as well. Btw, I had a nasty bug bite the other week. I had some left over lemon pulp. I squeezed some juice and left some pulp on it for a few minutes. The bite swelled down and didn't itch at all. Another great discovery with lovely lemons:) The tree-ripened and organic lemons I noticed has more seeds than the conventional ones. I gathered the seeds, dehydrated them and blended them into powder. Great way to add more potent C to food and beauty products.

Thanks Jim for all the info. I'm experimenting with different ways to make home-made products, remedies and food with all the various protocols you recommended. I wonder if moringa powder can work well topically???

Cheers! Joyce M.

A Word on diet:

So my advice here is to take the highest level foods and water possible as Joyce above is working toward.

Obviously, avoid ingesting low frequency drinks like commercial soft drinks ever. And, mostly, for those who will miss them, alcoholic drinks as the metylation therapists tell us.

Finally, the important thing here is know what to avoid and what the levels of positive and negative effects are.

With this information, as you play this checker game of life, you know what each move entails. As this level of study goes on, this information will become available if it is used correctly.

Levels of Wellness: A New Realization

With the writing of this book, I came to a new realization that had not previously crossed my mind. It goes like this:

From the physical standpoint, there is a progression of wellness. In this, if we just look at the state of the body, rather than the names and descriptions placed on it by modern medicine, we see a progressive level of wellness occurring.

From highest to lowest, I describe these physical states (herein and in my previous book) as follows:

First, we have what Dan Nelson describes as the "God

Eaters." These, most will tell you, are mythical people, but from the standpoint of quantum physics, they exist. Also, the high spiritual masters speak of them and they appear in religious texts. They are people who live off the vibratory frequencies of food rather than physical food. How they manage this is well beyond our understanding, but I do believe that they can exist just from what I have learned in the past few years. Assuming that they do, if people need not digest food, they conserve the great deal of energy that goes into the conversion process and also avoid the chemicals that we must contend with in modern societies. So this would be the ideal state if achieved.

Next we have those who process their food on the ketogentic level. This is described by Dr. Attia and Mercola in the following video presentation and discussion (also on p.60 herein): http://www.lewrockwell.com/2014/02/Joseph-mercola/slow-aging-to-a-crawl-and-shrink-your-waist In this state, the human body no longer needs or craves sugar. Thus, it has moved to the highest known digestive state. As I say herein, I believe that Dr. Attia has gone too far in his choices and that his total avoidance of fruits with their magic phytochemicals is taking it too far. Dr. Mercola basically agrees in his commentary. Still this level is quite high compared to the population as a whole, and it should avoid the states that medicine described as "diseased" in this progression.

Next, we have the Low Carb Diet. This is well discussed

elsewhere, but it allows fruits as long as we stay within reason and attempts to avoid all pastry, bread, and pasta, again, within reason. That is, occasionally, you might eat a roll-up hand-out at a party, but never sit down for a dinner of pizza or spaghetti. I hold that this is the most reasonable level, believing that Dr. Attia is stressing his body with his level of eating. From an epigenetic standpoint, this is probably far more important than the actual food that he ingests. Also, his exercises appear to be quite stressful. The point here is that enjoyment of life is a valuable health factor and too much stress kills.

Then we have the transitional state that most Americans survive in today. It generally lasts about forty to fifty years before we slip into one of the states below. It relies on the nutrients that our mothers give us at birth, combined with a compromised amount of vitamins, minerals, essential fats and proteins. Once we cross the line nutritionally, we move into one of the preconditions below and finally succumb to one of them or a combination as our body's succumb.

Progressing down the scale, we have what modern medicine calls Type II Diabetes. This is one result of the Standard American Diet (SAD) and where a large segment of the population rests today, as it is more sustainable than the last. With the chemicals, sugars, etc., they no longer get the energy out of their foods that people once did. With this comes the digestive and elimination problems, and a host of others. Excess sugar is a poison, yet our population is taught to love it. Current science describes this as a "progressive disease," calling it, adult onset diabetes. "Sugar Diabetes," the previous term, was a better description. However, it does not sell the sugar laden foods as well and that is important to the industry.

No one sees a cure for it and given the foods that our population as a whole eats, they are correct. Because these people are literally starving, they are hungry, overweight, and thirsty. Beyond this, they have eye and circulation problems, which can result in blindness, heart disease, and the loss of limbs. Since this normally does not include an invasive species, I see diabetes as a normal progression in our population and not a disease. Also, the population disease rate is increasing alarmingly and for no popular or expressed reason, by current science.

Next we have what is termed as heart disease. It too is not caused by an outside invader. In this condition, as medical science correctly tells us, the circulatory system becomes brittle and thus the heart is overloaded with excess blood pressure. The condition is lethal, but it is easily dealt with if the person changes to the LCD and gets enough of the proper nutrients into the system. The primary ones lacking are organic sulfur and magnesium, but others complement them. This is probably a less systemic problem than diabetes, but is the major killer.

Finally, we have the cancerous state. This, in my opinion, is the weakest of all bodily states in this downward progression.

In this state, I submit, the body has become weakened by outside chemicals which may be in combination with a poor diet or an invasive species further adding to the progression.

However, the contention here is that cancer begins at the liver. The liver is the central processing plant for all energy production and our waste treatment plant. If it becomes overloaded, it sends the offending problem to selected areas of the body, generally in packets (tumors), in an effort to preserve its existence.

A healthy body sees any offending cells and removes them with its immune system, but in this weakened state it cannot. If the above diabetic state or cancer is combined with an invasive species, that is, a virus such as Lymes or a nanobacteria, the combination can be particularly lethal as the immune system becomes doubly taxed. In fact, as several doctors have contended, and Royal Rife, in the '30's proved, once an offending virus is removed, people generally become cancer free.

What We Now Know

What epigentics teaches related to the above is that each of the above states is a choice, whether or not it is rational, even though our government (the FDA) and healthcare system disagrees. Again, there are no victims. However, if you are unaware of what is occurring, you might swear that you are the result of bad genes or even bad luck. Dr. Attia, an oncologist, may still believe that genes are involved, but he now knows that you can play the diet card your way and avoid these last states.

So What is Sacred? How It All Ties Together.

I have been reporting on the works of Dr. Bruce Lipton here as a result of my learning about the new sciences of Epigenetics, Cellular Microbiology, and the Methylation Sequences for about a year. His work, in my opinion, stands out when you look at what he offers in cellular biology. His creative conclusions take him to the spiritual truth, "We are the masters of our fate, not victims..." So big pharma does not control us and neither does the AMA. This understanding begins to cross the barrier between science and spirituality. Spirituality, based on unconditional love is, in my opinion, the highest truth and, by extension, the most powerful healer. Lipton with epigentics takes us to the same conclusion, but herein, my point is that both are limited. This epigenetic science, just a few years since its invention, is the most cutting edge of scientific knowledge out there today. The most exciting part of this, to me, is that it is proving repeatable and is thus taking its place among the mainstream as time goes on. With it, we can prove that the mind is a far more powerful healer than any medicine.

There are problems with what Lipton tells us, however. Once anything is written or spoken, it is no longer spiritual. Why? Because spirituality is never frozen in time. As soon as something becomes "common knowledge," it is frozen, it takes its place in this reality. So what this is saying is that even what we consider as sacred is mental and not if you equate the spiritual to sacred as I do here. Furthermore, all sacred books are written. Therefore, they are also frozen in time. What Bruce has revealed is not sacred and he clearly sees the unconscious mind as the highest knowledge. A new understanding of love is indeed sacred until revealed. However, as soon as we reveal a dream or revelation to another, it loses power, it becomes common knowledge. Thus, it is frozen in time and subject to religious beliefs. Spirit (cause) is constantly at work in our lives. It is timeless, always loving, and all powerful.

We, as the spiritual entities that inhabit our bodies, generally want to see proofs and logic in our lives. Therefore, science will always have its place among us. The illusion is that science is reality and spirituality is illusion. Herein, I submit that the opposite is always true.

While not endorsing any religion here, the Jewish notion that God's face can never be shown, takes the above timeless notion into account. However, in the same breath, they tell us that their writings and their bible is sacred. By their correct first notion, their second is incorrect. Thus, I must add a third qualification (even though spirituality can never really be qualified); once you materialize spirit in any way, the love is lost because it becomes fixed in time.

So the underlying truth here is that Love can never be confined, or even defined, because "It" must remain free to change as your understanding and awareness of love grows. However, you can read what you consider a sacred work, take it within, visualize a result, emote a sacred thought, and take it even further. Since love is timeless, this is a never ending sequence. This is love in action and it is the essence of your very beingness, that spiritual entity commonly termed as Soul.

So bringing what Lipton brings into the above defined term is with his, "Biology of Change" book, **https://www.brucelipton.com/books/biology-of-belief** and video, **https://www.youtube.com/watch?v=jjj0xVM4x1I**.

Why? Because Lipton's conclusion frees us from the chains of materialism and with that, the victim consciousness. Thus, his creativity is seldom matched in all of science, ever. However, he always stops, and must, at the subconscious level, which he defines as the automatic action that we all engage in if we are to exist.

Dr. Rob Williams, on this same above tape, also must stop with the subconscious level. Herein, and correctly, within his confines, he speaks of a Subconscious mind that "knows" current conditions. From here, he goes on to teach the art of dowsing. In this case, of using muscle tests. But generally all of this is considered pseudoscience garbage by the mainstream. While muscle tests are generally accurate, in my experience, they depend on current conditions, because as spiritual beings we can change conditions in a heartbeat. However, this seldom occurs. Why? Because most of us are bound and firmly rooted in time. That is, what we commonly call physical reality. What is this physical reality? The illusion that we are under the chains of those who control us and the rules that time hold. As we cross the high spiritual divide called the fifth plan or dimension, the rules all change. However, no one gains access to that level without an earned pass, a pass that a high degree of awareness and love yields.

So when we get to Dr. Lipton's book, The Honeymoon Effect, **https://www.youtube.com/watch?v=JKe43Ak1y1c** we see that Bruce has defined love strictly as sexual love. However, once you define love, you have limited your understanding. So what he tells us appears to be true, and it is great fun, but it is no longer correct.

Love is unlimited and timeless. Being unlimited, our understanding of it changes as we grow spiritually. Certainly, sexual love could be unlimited to a degree and timeless, but there is more, much more. Still, what Lipton and Williams teach on their video lectures is a new milestone that moves science far up the bar. Presently, then, we must accept this limited understanding of a love, somewhat trapped in time, even though they must define the subconscious as timeless outer boundary.

The point here is that there are spiritual levels far more esoteric and beyond what Lipton's science, books, and videos teach and this level transcends the subconscious mind, anything material, space, time, and even thought. However, this new science of epigenetics is still a giant step beyond the science of the past and that is the point of this final Chapter.

Printed in Great Britain
by Amazon